tALKING PICTURES

How to turn a trip to the movies into a mission trip

Jacob Youmans

TRI-PILLAR PUBLISHING

TALKING PICTURES

Tri-Pillar Publishing
Anaheim Hills, California
Website: www.TriPillarPublishing.com
e-mail: tripillarpublishing@cox.net

International Standard Book Number --13:   978-0-9818923-2-0

International Standard Book Number --10:   0-9818923-2-9

Library of Congress Catalog Card Number: 2010929899

First edition, June, 2010

Printed in the United States of America

Contents

Acknowledgments

To quote Hannibal from *The A-Team*, "I love it when a plan comes together!"

And with this book in particular, I thank God that it was His plan. It certainly wasn't *my* plan – and thank God for that! Without Him, none of this would have happened. This plan has played out over years and years, and with more people and movies than I can count. Movies and ministry just always seemed to go hand in hand for me.

There are so many people to thank and acknowledgments to give.

I need to thank my parents, Kim and Sandra Youmans, for taking me to the movies as a kid and teaching me the power of stories. I also want to thank my brothers, Andrew and Nathan, and my sister Naomi for making the movies come alive in our play as kids – and always letting me be Luke Skywalker.

Thanks so much to Josephine, Andy, and Peter Dibble at Tri-Pillar Publishing for believing in this book and the ministry that will come from it. You have been a tremendous blessing! You have pushed me and forced me to stretch and grow as a writer. God really brought you into my life at the perfect time! Thank you so much!

Thanks to all of my former students and coworkers at Our Savior Lutheran Church in Aiea, Hawaii, and St. Paul's Lutheran Church in Orange, California, for being the "guinea pigs" for so many of these ideas and concepts. Thanks for your love and support even as miles and time separate us.

Thanks to Josh Tinney for being our "fact checker." I am so excited to watch God at work as you start your professional ministry!

Thanks to Rev. Terry O'Brien and Heath Trampe for their excellent work as theological advisors and editors. I greatly appreciate the time and effort you gentlemen put in to make sure that Christ is proclaimed in His truth and entirety on every page!

To Dr. Leonard Sweet – I cannot give you enough credit for inspiring me to keep pushing in ministry. The night I asked you why you were still a Methodist and your appropriate response has done more to keep me in the Lutheran Church than anything else. Thank you for being one of my mentors.

As this book goes to print, it will be published right around our 12th year wedding anniversary. My beautiful wife, Christy, has put up with way more than anyone can understand these past 12 years. With 3 moves, 2 kids, and 8 years of going to school full time and working full time, it's been quite an adventure. I love you Christy! I hope you see your heart and passion for the lost on the pages of this book. Life with you is better than any life in the movies!

To my daughters Maile and Leilani – you inspire me every day! Jesus told His disciples that they will do greater things then this, and I believe with all my heart that you both will do incredible things for Jesus and His Kingdom! I am so proud of you and love you so much! And of course, remember that Jesus loves you even more than Daddy!

Finally, thank you, Jesus, for bringing this plan together in Your perfect time!

Foreword

"We've got the syrup, but it doesn't pour."[1]

These words were written by the 20th century American writer Gertrude Stein, who was born in Pennsylvania but lived most of her life in Paris. Stein was as well known for her friendships with artists like Picasso, Matisse, and Hemingway as for her own art.

The challenge of evangelism is encapsulated in that phrase: "We've got the syrup, but it doesn't pour." The Gospel sweetness is rich and ambrosial. The problem is we don't know how to pour.

To pour syrup, you need to do three things. First, you must tilt it on its side. Syrup comes out sideways – not straight up. The flow comes from a sideways slant, or as Emily Dickinson put it, "Tell all the truth, but tell it slant."[2]

Second, you must actually tumble the insides out. To pour means to stream or flow continuously or profusely. This always involves some shaking and some spillage. Assuming you have the proper vessel, the amount of sticky messiness left behind will be minimal. But in pouring out and not keeping in, there will always be spillage.

Third, you need heat. Whether the heat is supplied by the warmth of spring that releases the syrup into an empty bucket from the opening in the bark once the tree has been tapped – or whether the heat is supplied by the fire from a stove or the warmth of a hand – there is no pouring without some heat. Interestingly, the greater the heat under the syrup, the easier it is to pour initially but the thicker the syrup eventually becomes.

There is only one way to bypass these three steps. What if we were so powerfully filled to overflowing with the sweetness of the Spirit that the tipping and tapping and temping from the outside are no longer issues?

Nothing pours syrup better than cinema, which is why I am so excited about Jacob Youmans's book. I was a long time coming to a celluloid life. As a child, my brothers and I weren't permitted to go to the movies because my mother believed cinema was mind molestation; seeing images of violence or rebellion could cause juvenile delinquency or worse, e.g., parental defiance. But I learned in Mother's critique of movies that an ethic of images is as morally significant as an ethic of words. Just as there are certain words you should never say (and if you do, there are cleansing rituals to purify the mouth and mind), so there are certain images you should never see. Images have power to shape reality – so much, in fact, that movies invariably end up #1 on the lists of things that influence us and shape our destiny (followed by television, music, the Internet, books, parents, sports figures, etc.).[3]

Don't believe me? You kiss the way you do because of motion pictures. Movies fetishized kisses, which historians tell us were never so prolonged (or wet) in previous centuries as they have been since *The Kiss* (1896). (This film, one of the first ever shown, is just 47 seconds long, making it a short kiss by today's standards.) Or just ask the Mafia, which has been as much created by, as inspirer of, movies. In New York City, the Mafia was basically washed up in the early 1970s. Then *The Godfather* came out in 1972 and told them who they were – not thugs, but a new generation of immigrants out to get their piece of the American pie and to make the dream of the Promised Land come true. Thus began their comeback. The mafiosi got new life as they attempted to look and act like their screen images.

But the pouring power of movies was brought home to me in the first movie I ever saw. I can still remember the naughty excitation of sneaking out of the house to go to a movie after screwing up my courage by listening to the Beach Boys song "Good Vibrations." I had no idea what was playing, and found myself at the premier showing of Michelangelo Antonioni's *Blowup* (1966). A photographer played by David Hemmings accidentally captures with his camera what appears to be a murder in a London park. But when he tries to enlarge the shots, the images get cloudy and blurred. The photographer learns that we see what we want to see, or what we are trained to see, or what we believe we see – a message reinforced by an unforgettable tennis match played without a ball at the conclusion of the movie.

I shall never forget that one film's powers over me of tipping, tilting, and temping. Pablo Picasso was talking of all art when he said, "Art is a lie that makes us realize the truth."[4] But the ability of *Blowup* to defamiliarize the familiar, and to make me see that looking itself was subjective and partial and contextual, is a lesson I've never forgotten. The need for life to be constantly tilting, pouring, and in motion, and the inability of still photography to capture truth has stayed with me – even in the form of a prejudice against still life paintings. Finally, I found myself so heated up about the movie that I couldn't stop talking about it. I encouraged all of my friends to go see it so we could compare notes and talk about it together.

Unwittingly I had become an evangelist, and to this day I use enthusiasm for a good movie as a distinction between an evangelism of invitation and an evangelism of imposition. To share your excitement over a movie or book you've enjoyed is not to impose your judgments on anyone; but it is to invite them to share your joy with you.

Also unwittingly, I had become a cinephile, and toyed mischievously as a teenager with the idea of becoming a film critic. To this day, I can't imagine a life without movies any more than a room without windows. Movies are apertures and avenues of escape to the soul, vistas that scan other scenes and screens, where the mind may alight and find delight and freshening. Movies are sanctuaries for the lonely, way stations for the weary, neutral gears for the racing mind, and time capsules for the constrained and confined.

In the history of art, Christian themes have dominated every art form except photography, cinema, and social networking. But even though the world isn't making it easy for us, this book provides practical, hands-on strategies for showing how films can help people invite others into a relationship with Christ, and how films can help people discover their own stories of despair, illness, and loneliness as we connect them to biblical stories of healing and salvation that pull them toward Jesus and recovery.

St. Brendan the Voyager, a wandering Irish preacher and monastic, had been talking to Brude, one of the early kings of Scotland, about Christ and what it meant to follow Jesus. The king asked Brendan: "What shall I find if I accept your Gospel and become Christ's man?" The old saint replied, "O King, if you become Christ's man, you will stumble on wonder upon wonder, and every wonder true."[5]

Wonder upon wonder, and every wonder true…

The book you are holding can help you pour the sweet wonder of that syrup to your family, friends, and community.

Leonard Sweet

---

[1] The actual quote is "He has a certain syrup but it does not pour," *Selected Writings of Gertrude Stein*, (New York: Vintage Books, 1990), 206. Stein said this of American novelist Glenway Westcott.

[2] Emily Dickinson, "Tell All the Truth," in *The Complete Poems of Emily Dickinson*, ed. Thomas H. Johnson (Boston: Little, Brown, 1960), 506.

[3] George Barna calls these "SSI" or Strategic Sources of Influence. By the way, the Church either doesn't appear on his list or is way, way down the list.

[4] Pablo Picasso, *Picasso on Art: A Selection of Views*, comp. Dore Ashton (New York: Viking Press, 72), 21. (bao)

[5] Quoted in Billy Graham, *Blow Wind of God: Selected Writings of Billy Graham*, ed. Donald E. Demarary (Old Tappan, NJ: Revell, 1977), 73.

Introduction

The Three Questions

Question #1
How Many Movies Do You Watch in a Week?

How many movies, on average, do you watch in a week? Have you ever really thought about it? There are nearly unlimited movie choices today, in many different genres: major Hollywood hit blockbusters, edgy and trendy independent films, action/adventure, romance, westerns, science fiction, horror, mystery/suspense, comedy, drama, and documentary. And it seems like there are a gazillion more choices every day! Do you realize that even if you watched one movie a day for a year, you wouldn't be able to watch all the movies that are released this year? Movies, movies everywhere. How many do you watch in a week?

Now before you answer, don't just think about the movies you've seen while sitting in the plush, comfortable seats of a state-of-the-art movie theater with a warm bucket of golden buttery popcorn and an ice cold Cherry Coke®. Don't forget about the movies you watch on TV, DVD, HD-DVD, Blu-ray™, your computer, and even your video iPod™. Movies can be seen everywhere – from the neighborhood multiplex to the two-inch video iPod nano™ screen.

I was at the dentist recently, and while he worked on my teeth, he put these "magic" goggles on me and I could watch pretty much any movie I wanted. No more trying to talk with his hands in my mouth. I was able to just sit back, relax, and enjoy the show. Movies are available on the go like never before. You can choose a new release from a DVD vending machine in your local grocery store while you're there picking up something for dinner. What's more, movie rental companies don't even need or expect you to come into a store anymore; you just make an online list of all the movies you want to see and they'll send the movies to you in the mail. (Looks like the U.S. Postal Service "snail mail" is still good for something!) Adding all of these up, how many movies *do* you watch in an average week?

According to the website, www.answerbag.com, "The number of films the average American watches all together, including rentals, movies at home, cinemas, and movies at friend's houses, would be a nearly impossible number to find." This isn't Mission Difficult, my friends – it's Mission Nearly Impossible! I don't think even Tom Cruise himself could help us figure out the answer to a question like this. Needless to say, we all watch a lot of movies!

But what is it about movies that attracts us so irresistibly? Since Thomas Edison first invented the motion picture machine (yes, the light bulb guy also invented the movie!) way back in the late 1800s, the popularity of movies has skyrocketed. Movies are everywhere. Movie stars and characters grace everything from toothpaste tubes to lunch boxes. Movies are turned into video games and theme park attractions.

Did you know that American-made movies are one of our most profitable, and controversial, exports to the rest of the world? Hollywood is capitalizing on the globalization of the movie business by releasing movies all over the world on the very same day. In the very recent past, only a limited number of Hollywood movies would be released in foreign countries, and this would occur long after the U.S. release. I was in New Zealand when *Pirates of the Caribbean: Dead Man's Chest* came out, and we couldn't get tickets for it.

Every show was sold out for two weeks. Captain Jack Sparrow strikes again!

People all over the world are watching American movies every day, believing that what they see on the silver screen is how life really is for those fortunate, spoiled citizens of the United States of America. Some people in the world despise *all* Americans due to what they see in our movies and popular culture. Much has been said about the hatred from Muslim extremists for Western culture, largely due to our popular culture exports and the morals and values portrayed in them. Other foreigners are so impressed by what they see in our films that they pick up and move to the U.S., hoping to live the dream life of their favorite characters in the movies. My own mother-in-law immigrated to America with her new Air Force Airman husband and was extremely disappointed that the United States of America did not look more like what she saw in the movies while growing up. Movies have power! How many movies do you see in a typical week?

Question #2
Do You Watch Movies Alone or with Others?

Be honest, now… do you watch the majority of those movies all by your lonesome, curled up on the couch, wearing your *High School Musical* pajamas? Or do you tend to view your movies with family and friends – the people who really matter to you?

I held a wide variety of odd jobs in high school. But my absolute favorite high school job was working at the beautiful Red Rock Theater in Las Vegas, Nevada. The original theater doesn't exist anymore, because they tore it down a while back. But I sure have a lot of great memories of that place! That's where my fascination of the power of movies was born.

I did it all at the theater: selling tickets; ripping tickets; making and serving popcorn, snacks and beverages; cleaning the theaters; starting the movie; ushering people in and out of the theater; kicking out kids that snuck in or theater-hopped. I was a movie theater employee machine! They asked if they could clone me to create the ultimate employee team, but I respectfully declined. While working at that theater, I made a lot of friends, ate way too much popcorn, drank too much soda, and got a bunch of free movie posters and memorabilia. Most importantly, I got to watch a ton of movies for my favorite price – free!

During the time I spent working at my beloved movie theater, I noticed a near-universal trend – almost no one goes to the movies alone. Sometimes it's a couple, but most often it's a group experience. Movie time is a time to connect with other people. You may not utter a single word to each other for two hours (unless it's "excuse me" when you need to get up to go to the bathroom), but you're connecting nonetheless through the shared movie experience. Movies are much more fun in a packed theater, where everyone understands the inside jokes, and people seem to know when to laugh and when not to laugh.

I really enjoy going to the midnight premiers of the big blockbusters. Everyone who's there *really* wants to be there, and they immerse themselves in the overall motion picture experience. You don't go to a movie at midnight unless you're dying to see it! Many of these midnight moviegoers even come in costume. While seeing the second *Star Wars* Trilogy at midnight, I've sat near several Wookiees, Darth Vader, Princess Leia (who wasn't even in those movies!), folks with lightsabers and of course guys sporting the very cool ancient "Jedi ponytails." I saw *Indiana*

Jones and the Kingdom of the Crystal Skull at midnight and I felt very much out of place without a fedora or a whip.

The moviegoing experience is usually more memorable when you have friends and family to be amused, scared, shocked, moved, laugh, or maybe even cry with. I'm not trying to imply that you're weird if you choose to go to a movie theater alone; you're just in the minority. I still remember who was with me when I saw certain movies many years ago. Seeing movies with friends is a way to make lasting memories. Sometimes, who you go with is much more memorable then the movie itself!

Question #3
Do You Talk about Movies?

When the closing credits roll, do you find yourself talking to your companions about what you just experienced? Reflecting back on my days of wearing the sharp black vest and crisp bow tie at the local multiplex, I observed that while exiting a movie theater, most people talk to the people around them about what they just experienced together. Movies are social events, and there are perhaps few discussion-starters that are more natural.

The legacy of movie critics Gene Siskel and Roger Ebert is that we have all been taught how to talk intelligently about movies. We've learned how to be movie critics as well, giving a movie a "thumbs up" or "thumbs down," a passing or failing grade, or a certain number of stars. Movies spark conversations, discussions, and debates, as everyone tends to develop an opinion very quickly. I was speaking at a youth gathering not too long ago, and for the first time I had a young lady tell me that she wanted to go to college to become a movie critic. A *movie critic*! She was the first person I ever met who seriously wanted to critique movies for a living. Not that many years ago, few people would have ever thought of becoming a movie critic as a full time profession. Sure, the job existed, but there were not nearly as many movie critics as there are today.

A lot of people will even talk to complete strangers after they have seen a movie together. But, let's face it, after sitting through a movie together, are you still "strangers?" You now have a common bond through the shared movie experience. Whether you've just been through a 1½-hour animated feature or a 3-hour epic science fiction adventure, you've just got to talk about it with someone!

Have you ever been to a movie on a first date? I think most of us have, and there's a very good reason why a movie is a great setting for a first date. No matter how comfortable or uncomfortable you are, it gives you both something to talk about. The irony, of course, is that we're not supposed to talk during a movie. Trust me – I've been loudly "shhhhhed" quite a few times! And yet talking and movies go hand in hand.

So think through these questions…

- How many movies do you watch in a week?
- Do you watch movies alone or with others?
- Do you talk about movies?

Pray about It

- Pray for how God might use this book in your life.

Talk about It

- Think about your favorite movies. What makes them your favorites?

- What do your favorite movies have in common? How are they different?

- Who do you tend to go to movies with? Do they know Jesus as Lord and Savior? How do you know for sure?

- What do you and your friends talk about after seeing a movie? Do you see how that conversation could become spiritual?

Live It Out

- Make a list of three friends who don't yet know Jesus as Lord and Savior. Would these friends be open to talking about spiritual things? Would they go to a movie with you? Pray regularly for these friends, and for opportunities to share the love of Christ with each of them.

Talking Pictures Example #1

As we left the darkened theater after seeing *The Dark Knight*, one thought was consuming my mind and I just had to say it. "Heath Ledger was incredible! The Joker stole the show!"

"Yeah!" agreed my friend Steve. "He was pure evil. I've actually read that it was this role that made him take the medication that eventually killed him. He was having nightmares from this role! Scary!"

"And the Joker didn't really have any reason to be evil," I added. "Nothing really motivated him to be that way – he just was."

"No kidding! Good thing that's just a movie. In real life, there's always a reason someone turns out bad."

"You really think so?" I wondered aloud, encouraging him to explain.

"Oh, yeah," Steve replied. "Human beings are naturally good, and it takes a bad experience or a tragedy to turn them evil."

"Huh," I said thoughtfully, as if I was pondering what he had said. After a pause, I continued. "Well, I wish that was true, but I know plenty of people who just do evil stuff for no real reason. I wish people were naturally good. But when I see wars, abuse of power, enslavement, and poverty consuming the world, I'm not convinced that people are naturally good."

"What do you mean?" Steve turned toward me, clearly interested in my statement. I began to realize that a window of opportunity was starting to open up. You see, Steve wasn't a Christian, and I had always wanted to find a good time to work the topic of my faith into one of our conversations. I knew this might be the opportunity I had been waiting for.

"Well," I said, taking a deep breath and saying a silent prayer, "Everyone has evil thoughts. Everyone has a natural desire to do bad things. This guy, Paul, who wrote a bunch of books – well, more like letters – he was frustrated by this whole issue too. In fact, he put it this way: 'The good I want to do, I *don't* do, but the bad I don't want to do, this I *do.*'"

"Paul sounds like an evil guy!" Steve said quickly, and then asked, "So what bad stuff did he do?"

"He *was* evil!" I agreed. "In fact, he was a sort of hit man for an ancient Mafia-type group. He was a pretty bad dude. But something crazy and unexpected happened to him." I knew that I had Steve's interest now.

"What happened?" he asked eagerly. "Did he get whacked?"

"He got whacked off his donkey!" I smiled, knowing that he wouldn't quite get the joke. "He had an encounter that forced him to change."

"He got arrested? Did he go into the witness protection program? Was he a rat?" Steve was anxious to find out more.

"No, he wasn't arrested. But he *was* convicted," I said. "He was shown the evil of his ways and given a second chance."

"Huh?" Steve said, not really sure what to say next. He was quiet as we walked back to the car and got inside. As we started driving away, I wondered if I had lost the conversation. But then he said thoughtfully, "Well, you gotta love a second chance. So, what happened to him after that?"

Relieved that I still had his interest and curiosity, I knew that I could keep going with the topic. "Well, Paul took full advantage of that second chance. His life turned completely around. In fact, many consider him to be one of the most important people who ever lived! He took this news about a second chance to the whole world. We all need a second chance."

"What news about a second chance?" he asked.

"Jesus." I paused for a moment and saw him nodding thoughtfully. I continued to explain. "Paul developed a relationship with Jesus, and Jesus gave him a second chance. It's not that Paul became perfect, but he did take full advantage of that second chance. He was so grateful he had the opportunity to see the light, and he spent the rest of his life doing great things. He traveled all over the place and told everyone they also could have a second chance in Jesus. He was even thrown in jail for telling everyone about Jesus, but God broke the locks and chains off of him and set him free!"

"Hey, you said he wrote letters about it, right?" Steve asked. "Can I read those sometime? That's quite a story."

The Evangelist/Translator

What's This Book About?

The title of this book, *Talking Pictures*, is meant to be a play on words. The first films to have sound came out in the 1920s and were called "talking pictures." The goal of this book is to teach and encourage people to use movies as a way to initiate conversations with others about the grace given to us through Jesus. You can use the natural power of movies, and the fascination we have for them, to talk about your faith and the power and glory of God working in your life.

Yes – believe it or not, God can use all these post-movie discussions and chit-chat to His glory! Your conversations about movies give you a huge opportunity to see Jesus in, with, and under the celluloid film – and, more importantly, show Him to your friends and acquaintances who don't yet know Jesus as Lord and Savior.

Throughout this book, I will be referencing movies and quoting movie lines. Many of the movies mentioned are well-known blockbusters that you've seen and loved, while others you may not be as familiar with. This is intentional. This isn't a book about your, or even my, favorite movies. This isn't a book on how to talk to your friends about Jesus after watching a Jesus movie. This book isn't "The Gospel According to *Harry Potter*," "... *Star Wars*," "... *The Simpsons*," etc. I want to show you that just about any movie can stir up conversations that, by God's grace, can ultimately point back to Jesus. This method of witnessing is what I will be referring to, throughout this book, as Talking Pictures.

Those conversations we share after a movie can actually be turned into... get ready for it... EVANGELISM! Does that word send shivers down your spine, like when the hyenas in *The Lion King* hear Mufasa? Well, it doesn't have to be a nerve-wracking experience. My goal is to show you in the pages to follow that evangelism can be as simple as taking a friend to a movie and talking about it. That simple trip to the local multiplex could very well turn into a mission trip, and might provide you with some of the most effective witnessing opportunities of your life. Imagine that! You don't have to travel all the way to Africa to go on a mission trip.

I completely understand if you're a little scared or intimidated by the idea of evangelism. All of us are, at first. I certainly was, and I'm still nervous about it at times. We have such a strong desire to fit in, blend in, and find the happy medium between being noticed and being part of the crowd. We want people to like us and accept us. We don't want to be labeled as a "Jesus Freak." Then how do we comfortably witness to our friends, family and coworkers? Is it possible to be "normal" and be evangelistic? It may seem easier to say nothing than to go out on a limb. After all, we might be ridiculed, rejected, argued with, or shunned. But evangelism is serious and important stuff. We're talking about eternity here!

Ultimately, I believe our fear of evangelism is a fear of rejection – and a fear of failure. But we can't let fear control us. Angels said it; Jesus said it: "Fear not!" The funny thing about fear is that while we tend to think of it as a negative emotion, there are times when we purposely seek it out. People go to certain movies for the sole purpose of being scared out of their wits! Horror movies are popular because it can be fun to be scared and safe at the same time. We all know how good it feels to face our fears head-on and conquer them, and to realize that reality isn't nearly as bad as what we had imagined. Perhaps our fear of evangelism can actually motivate us to face the adventure that lies ahead. It can be scary to risk the ridicule of others, but we also know that we are safely in the arms of Jesus, and as St. John said, **"the one who is in you is greater than the one who is in the world."** (1 John 4:4)

In the movie *The Game Plan*, Dwayne "The Rock" Johnson is a star football quarterback who finds himself forced into a custody battle over his daughter. His daughter's ballet teacher (and his love interest) reminds him of the importance of a father's role with these words: "Fathers give us courage to do things we don't think we can do." That's exactly what your Heavenly Father is going to do with you in your role as an evangelist[1]. He's going to give you the courage you need to tell the whole world about His everlasting love. You don't have to worry about whether you can do it. God will give you the courage! Throughout the Old Testament, God calls His people to be strong and courageous. God will equip you with the strength and courage you need. Don't let your fears stop you. It's not about failure, because it's not about *us* – it's about God working *in* us and *through* us, and God doesn't fail! God says in Isaiah 55:11, **"my word that goes out from my mouth: It will not return to me empty, but will accomplish what I desire and achieve the purpose for which I sent it."** God's purposes are so much greater than ours, and God's purposes are always fulfilled.

Now, it's true that it's all about God and not you. But guess what? God wants to use *you* in the spiritual battle! Think about the story of David and Goliath. David prayed that God would defeat Goliath. Of course, we know that God, being almighty, could have accomplished this feat in any

---

[1] Throughout this book, I use the term "evangelist" and "witness" interchangeably. While we don't all have the spiritual gift of evangelism, we all play a role in evangelism when we witness.

number of ways. He could have caused Goliath to die in his sleep. He could have given him a heart attack or a stroke on the battlefield. God could have defeated him any way He wanted. But God chose to use David and to work through him to win the battle. God wants to work through you in the same way. He wants you to be engaged in the battle! (1 Timothy 6:12)

Wait a Minute!

By now, some of you may be thinking, "Wait a minute – how can we use movies as a means for evangelism when the vast majority of Hollywood movies don't have any obvious tie to Christianity at all?" That's an excellent question! Yes, you are correct. Not every movie is as blatantly, in-your-face Christian as *The Passion of the Christ,* or *The Nativity Story.* And not every movie has obvious spiritual connections that easily lead to deep conversations like *Fireproof, To Save a Life,* or *The Chronicles of Narnia: The Lion, the Witch and the Wardrobe.* These are all wonderfully made movies and God has certainly used them for His glory. But what about the other 99% of movies?

The fact is, many major motion pictures today seem to be made with a very different kind of "evangelism" in mind other than Christian. Movies can be very influential "evangelists" for premarital sex, drug use, violence, vulgarity, and all other sorts of things that are against God's plan for us. Movies such as *Natural Born Killers* and *The Basketball Diaries* have been listed in lawsuits for the murders they have allegedly inspired. The movie *The Program,* which is about a corrupt college football program, originally included a scene where the football team lays down in a busy street to prove their fearlessness. But in real life, a high school football team tried the same thing they saw in the movie, and a few kids died. Subsequently, that scene was cut from the movie. As a youth leader, I have had many students come to me and confess their unfortunate use of their sexuality. What is disturbing is that many of them admit that their choices were inspired and motivated by what they saw in a certain movie. When my wife and I have led couples through premarital counseling in the church, one of the things we make sure to tell each couple is that sex is not like the movies. Believe it or not, some couples are surprised by that!

When certain movies are released, like *Kiss the Girls*, or any of the horror genre known as "torture porn," such as *Saw* or *Hostel*, I worry that some people out there may watch those movies and think, "Hey, that's a great idea! I should try that!" The world is occupied by some very sick people. Evil is real. It should not be ignored or brushed off as "art." Some movies are made to shock and really have no redeeming or relatable value whatsoever.

Make no mistake – there are many things contained in movies that should give us cause for concern. Currently, many movies that are rated PG-13 are actually filthier than the previous generation of R rated movies. The goal of the filmmakers at times seems to be to push the limits of what the Motion Picture Association of America (MPAA) censors will allow. Today some PG-13 movies could be described as soft-core pornography, and some R rated movies blur the line between an R rating and blatant pornography.

Another concern is that many of the commercials and trailers for movies can be very misleading about the content of those films. The movie *Marley and Me* was advertised as a family-friendly movie about a difficult but lovable dog. My young daughters loved puppies, so we took them to see it. Unfortunately, after about 45 minutes of a movie that contained several sex scenes, Jennifer Aniston giving birth to a stillborn baby, and Owen Wilson's playboy best friend, we had to leave the theater. It was just not an appropriate movie for young kids, but the commercials made it look like it would be!

There are so many things to be concerned about in the unhealthy and blatantly anti-God morality portrayed in many major motion pictures. All too often, the characters in these movies aren't even remotely bothered by their sinful behavior, and often glorify it. However, as Christians, we should always remember that God does not take sin lightly. He tells us in Romans 6:23, **"For the wages of sin is death."** We should never accept or tolerate what is sinful. Sin is serious. It is so serious, in fact, that Jesus went to the cross and died to forgive us of our sins – many of which we don't even know we commit! There is no way to ever excuse sin. God doesn't, so we can't either. I believe that God can speak powerfully through any movie, but please choose your movies wisely. You don't want to lead your friend (or yourself) down a road of temptation and negative influences.

St. Paul gave some similar advice to his friends in Corinth who were wondering if it was okay to eat food sacrificed to idols. Paul made a very convincing argument in 1 Corinthians, chapter 8, that it was in fact all right to eat it. He explains that God is the one and only true God, and that sacrifices made to false gods are insignificant because those gods do not exist. But Paul goes on to remind us that the issue isn't as simple as eating versus not eating. He says in verse 9, **"Be careful, however, that the exercise of your freedom does not become a stumbling block to the weak."** Basically he is saying that we should not do anything, even those things that are not inherently sinful, that causes someone else to sin. Paul goes on to say in verse 13, **"if what I eat causes my brother to fall into sin, I will never eat meat again."** He's not joking around! Out of love for his brother, he would give up all meat so that no one would be able to ever accuse him of eating meat sacrificed to idols. He's completely above reproach.

So as you become more familiar with using movies as an evangelism tool, make sure the movies you are choosing don't lead anyone (yourself included) into sin. That would completely ruin the whole idea of what Talking Pictures is about – helping your friends come to know God and see Him at work in our world.

Omnimax® to Omnipresence

Here's an extremely important connecting point, and one that the whole concept of Talking Pictures hinges upon. One of our core beliefs as Christians is that God (Father, Son, and Holy Spirit) is omnipresent. Yes, God is truly everywhere at the very same time! The writer of Psalm 139 asks a great question: **"Where can I flee from your presence?"** (verse 7) Answer: NOWHERE! God is present everywhere. Try as we might, we cannot escape God's presence. We may be able to go *Back to the Future* with a flux capacitor, but our past, present, and future will all be played out in the presence of our almighty God. By the way, even a non-Christian's life is always within the sight and knowledge of God. God's presence isn't dependent upon your belief. He is always with us. We can't always see Him or feel His presence, but He is always there and He's always on duty, working His ultimate plan for humanity.

Check out Genesis chapter 3. Remember what happened to Adam and Eve in the Garden of Eden when they tried to flee God's presence? Their eyes were opened and they suddenly realized they were naked. They were ashamed, and their first reaction was the same as *Chicken Little* when he thought the sky is falling… RUN! However, like wise old Yoda said in *Star Wars: Episode V – The Empire Strikes Back*: "Do, or do not. There is no 'try.'" Don't try it; you cannot flee from the presence of God. God is everywhere.

St. Paul, while speaking in Athens, reminds us that **"in him (God) we live and move and have our being."** (Acts 17:28) That's a beautiful line, isn't it? By the way, Paul didn't make up that line himself. He is quoting first century pop culture – a poem written by a Cretan named Epimenides. And the quote was not even meant to be about God, Yahweh, the God of Abraham, Isaac, and Jacob. It was written about the Greek god Zeus! Yes, you read that right. Paul took something that was pagan, not intended to be about God, and used it to show who God is. He took something that was secular and explained how the sacred was in it. Paul himself found a way to be "Talking Poetry!" That would really impress the boys of the *Dead Poets Society*.

The line that the world has created dividing secular and sacred is simply not what God had intended for us. But in today's society we have movies and Christian movies. We have music and Christian music. This seems to happen primarily in the arts. For example, we don't have garbage men and Christian garbage men. We see more subdivision in the arts because they are such an expression of who we are and what we believe in.

In our society today, we seem to have made a sub-genre of our faith life. And yet in Jesus' time, all of life was considered a sacred gift from God because He is present in all things. Read some of the early books in the Old Testament: Leviticus, Numbers, and Deuteronomy. They contain detailed instructions on how to do such basic, everyday tasks as washing dishes, cleaning clothes, and maintaining proper diet and nutrition. They also give an account in painstaking detail on how to properly prepare your goat for sacrifice. Why were we given all of this instruction in such minute detail? Because all of life was understood to be sacred. God didn't intend for us to keep our faith in a drawer and only pull it out on Sunday morning along with our good church clothes. He wants our faith to be an active part of every moment of our lives, no matter where we are or what we are doing.

Do you find yourself acting differently at church on Sunday morning than you do during the rest of the week? Is your behavior different around your friends at school or work than it is with your church friends? Do you bounce back and forth between a secular and sacred life? I have to admit that there have been times when I've struggled with this myself. All of us are guilty, to some degree, of making this division in our lives. Why do we do that? For some of us, it might be the classic "everyone else is doing it" answer. Others may not have ever given much thought to their tendency to compartmentalize life. But when we are able to fully see God at work in the secular world, the dividing line between secular and sacred slowly begins to fade.

Due to the fall of humanity back in the Garden of Eden (Genesis 3), the world is now full of sin. As a consequence, we have the good and the bad mingled together in a way that's often confusing for us to navigate through. For this reason, we need to cling to the teaching of Jesus that His followers are *in* the world but not *of* the world (John 17:15-16). We still need to be involved in the world, but careful not to become consumed by it.

We must also remember that God can use for His glory even the things that were designed by human hands *not* to give Him glory. This is because, whether people realize it or not, God is still present. After all, human intentions are absolutely nothing compared to God's intentions, and God's ultimate intention is for all people to know Him! Remember John 3:16? **"For God so loved the world…"** The *whole* world? Wow, that's a lot of love!

This global message is communicated again in the book of Acts when Jesus says, **"But you will receive power when the Holy Spirit comes on you; and you will be my witnesses in Jerusalem, and in all Judea and Samaria, and**

to the ends of the earth." (Acts 1:8) Witnesses were a big deal in Jesus' time. The whole judicial system was built upon eyewitness accounts. There needed to be at least two eyewitnesses to convict a criminal. Witnesses were the way the ancient Jewish CSIs solved crimes. Witnesses were proof! You and your life are proof that Jesus is Lord. Remember that witnesses can be discredited by their mistakes and errors in judgment. People are watching if our words and our life line up properly. And no, you're not going to live perfectly... but live forgiven!

The whole-world theme is echoed again in 1 Timothy 2:3-4: **"God our Savior, who wants all men to be saved and to come to a knowledge of the truth."** How are people going to come to know the "knowledge of the truth?" That's where you enter center stage, my friend! You are the witness to the truth. You are the proof. And unlike Tom Cruise's character in *A Few Good Men*, you can indeed handle the truth.

In Scripture, God spoke through a burning bush, a donkey, a cloud, a small still voice, and a lot of very sinful people. So, I'm very confident that He can find a way to convey His message to the world using a Hollywood movie! Your mission is to help your unchurched friends see God's presence in the world around us, and watching the latest action-adventure flick together may be just the ticket to achieving this goal.

Me? A Translator?

Ah, I love the irony of it all... the Hollywood big-wigs and producers have no idea that God is actually using them to spread *His* message! God will always triumph over the sin and unbelief of this world. All that's needed is for you to "translate" the movie into God's Word. Interpret the eternal truths of God's Word into one of the common languages of our culture – movies.

Of all the things that Martin Luther (the main character in the cleverly titled movie *Luther*) did to change the world, perhaps the great reformer's most important work was translating the Holy Bible into German. German was the vernacular, or the common language, of the people that Luther ministered to. This translation was a monumental achievement because up until this point, the Bible was only available is Latin, Greek or Hebrew, and only the highly educated knew these languages. So the common man was left to trust that everything the priests said was actually from the Word of God. They could not check the Bible for themselves. The church at the time fought with great fervor against this change, because they literally controlled the minds and hearts of the people by controlling what people knew about the Bible. Like most political movements, it was all about power and control. However, we know that God is all about setting the captive free!

Luther was viewed as an outlaw. He was a wanted man with a huge price on his head for a good chunk of his life. But God worked through him to bring about powerful changes. For the first time in the history of the world, the inspired Word of God was in the common language. The mysteries of God were no longer chained to the libraries of the rich and educated. The Holy Scriptures now belonged to everyone!

When I was in Lutheran elementary school, it was a tradition every year on Reformation Day to watch an old 1950s movie based on the life of Martin Luther. Even in black-and-white, Luther manages to turn unmistakably red as he utters his famous line, "Unless proved by Scripture, I cannot recant these works!" By God's grace, Luther changed the world. Maybe you will, too!

Recall St. Paul in Athens. He cleverly used the altar of the unknown god as a "vernacular" of the Greek people. Read the story in Acts, chapter 17, starting at verse 16. The people worshiped numerous gods, yet were so afraid that they might forget about a god that they created a shrine to the unknown god, just to be on the safe side! Paul knew that the best way to connect with the people was through the things they already knew and understood. This is an effective method for us today as well. In order to share the life-changing news of the Gospel, we need to find ways to speak the common language of the people.

Recently, I had the privilege of preaching through an interpreter for the first time during a mission trip to work with the persecuted "underground" church in North Africa. It was an unforgettable experience. As I was speaking, I quickly realized that I really had no idea or control of what was going on. People laughed when I didn't think they were supposed to and they didn't laugh when I expected them to. I would say ten words and the translator would go on for ten minutes. I would then speak for several minutes and the translator would just say three little words. As uncomfortable and ineffective as it felt at times, this experience taught me the importance of a good translator.

Translators are vital. Without a translator, no one would understand what is communicated by the speaker. St. Paul calls for interpreters in 1 Corinthians 14. He reminds us in verse 5 that interpreters are essential, **"so that the church may be edified."** He even goes on to say in verse 11, **"If then I do not grasp the meaning of what someone is saying, I am a foreigner to the speaker, and he is a foreigner to me."** Interpreters are vital to the overall strength and health of the body of Christ, and for the growth of the church.

God is counting on you – yes, you! – to be His translator! Your calling[2] is one of an Evangelist/Translator. You're an E.T.! But if you think about it, that makes sense, because we are aliens in this world. Heaven is our home. And remember, it's pretty important to "phone home" regularly!

I know you probably never thought about being an Evangelist/Translator before, but whew, what a calling we have! People have been translating God's Word all over the globe for thousands of years. Whether it's making sense of a tribal language deep in the heart of Africa or sharing our faith with a friend while discussing a recent film, God's love through Jesus will be proclaimed in a way in which people understand. Perhaps through a movie, some people will hear the love of Jesus in their "language" for the very first time!

People often ask me what my favorite part of ministry is. I'd have to say that my favorite part is seeing that "Aha!" moment when the light bulb comes on. (Remember the light bulb guy also invented the movie!) When people realize exactly what Jesus has done for them, you can see the light bulb come on just like in a cartoon. It's the coolest thing in the world! Most of the M. Night Shyamalan movies have those light bulb moments when you figure out the twist. Bruce Willis is dead! Bruce Willis is *Unbreakable*. The aliens are leaving those *Signs* in the cornfields. *The Village* doesn't take place in Puritan times after all. In ministry, watching that light bulb of understanding come on is so rewarding. One student I worked with a while back summed it up perfectly: "If this Jesus stuff is true, then it's the most incredible thing ever!" Yes, it really is!

---

[2] Throughout this book, I use the term "call" not in reference to the divine call received by ordained clergy but rather in the sense that every Christian is "called" to spread the Gospel and reach out to others in love. I occasionally use the term "vocation" in the same sense.

Spectacular Vernacular

Vernacular – the common language we use to communicate with others – can be a funny thing. On a mission trip to Mexico, I had an encounter with a four-year-old boy named Victor. He was sitting all by himself, so I went up to him to try to befriend him. My Spanish is very poor, but I gave it a shot and attempted to speak to him in his native tongue. "¿Cómo te llamo?" I asked, which means, "What is your name?"

"Víctor," he said.

"¿Víctor?" I repeated.

"Sí."

"¡Excelente!" I said, wondering what I could say next. Hmm… oh, I know!

"¿Cuántos años?" I asked, which means, "How old are you?"

"Cuatro," he replied as he held up four fingers.

"¿Cuatro?"

"Sí."

"¡Excelente!" I exclaimed. Now, at this point I had completely run through the extent of my conversational Spanish. Fortunately, right at that moment, a dog ran across the parking lot. Excitedly, I pointed and said, "¡Víctor! ¡Perro, perro!"

"No!" he replied. "Doggy!"

I had thought that I was speaking Victor's vernacular, but evidently not! This is because vernacular isn't just about speaking a particular language. It's also about finding the *heart* language. It's about connecting to who people are and explaining things in a way they can understand and relate to. Remember that God's Word is meant for all the people of all the tribes and nations, and for all time.

But make no mistake about it – Bible translation can get pretty tricky. The key is to learn a new language and culture and apply God's eternal Word and truths to it. For example, how do you translate Psalm 51:7, **"I will be whiter than snow,"** to a tribe in the Amazon rain forest that has never seen a single snowflake? A friend of mine was a Bible translator in such a place and was faced with this very dilemma. He found a very white flower that was prominent in the area in which the tribe lived, and he told the people that Jesus would make their sins whiter than that flower. That's not exactly what Scripture says, but this certainly captures the spirit of what it is conveying.

For a great movie example of speaking the vernacular of the people, be sure to see *End of the Spear*. It's an independent movie about missionaries in Ecuador in the 1950s. Several missionaries were killed by this brutal tribe, the Waodani, who were known for their use of spears. The entire culture was saturated in death and violence. But the missionaries' children picked up the mantle of ministry and continued to bring God's Word and love to the tribe, even though these warriors had killed their parents. It's a great story of unconditional love in Jesus. The missionaries taught the Waodani the story of Jesus, using imagery that the tribe could understand. They talked about the "Great Chief's son," and they explained that He was loving and kind, but "they speared him, but he didn't spear them back." That's how they describe the crucifixion – as "spearing." But the people understood, and many of them are Christians to this day through the efforts of those missionaries!

We have to be creative with translating the Bible for different cultures. Jesus was! Do you think He would have said, **"Come, follow me... and I will make you fishers of men"** (Matthew 4:19) if He had been talking to businessmen, carpenters, or even religious leaders? He was talking to fishermen, and He used words and references that related to their livelihood. Jesus always knew the right words to use to reach each individual and group that He met. He told the rich young ruler to sell everything he had and give it all to the poor. (He didn't give those instructions to a poor guy!) Jesus told Nicodemus, one of the wisest men in Jerusalem, to be "**born again**" (John 3:3) and to forget all his knowledge and how smart he thinks he is. He didn't say this to a dumb guy – just one of the most educated men. Jesus spoke directly to the heart of the person. He reached in and touched his situation, his culture, and even his pride.

Jesus spoke in parables to speak right into the culture of the day. Parables are simply stories that people can easily relate to. Almost everyone in Jesus' day knew about sowers, mustard seeds, wedding banquets, Samaritans, and shepherds. Many of Jesus' parables start out with the phrase, "The Kingdom of God is like..." and then He would weave His tale. Maybe initiating a Talking Pictures conversation is as simple as using a similar phrase, such as "God's love is like...," "God's forgiveness is like...," "Grace is like...," and so on. Parables and movies really do have quite a bit in common. They are stories that connect to a culture.

American teenage life is a completely different sub-culture. It has its own language and communication styles, and it needs to hear the Word of God explained in that language. Talking Pictures is an effective way to accomplish that. If you are a teen, this is your chance to speak God's Word in the language of your people! You have a tremendous opportunity ahead of you. Did you know that back in the 1500s, people were burned at the stake for taking the Bible out of the original languages? But now, even teenagers can do it! You're a great reformer bringing God's Word to His people in a way they can understand.

It isn't always easy to see God at work in this complicated world of ours, and it isn't always going to be clear and straightforward to see God at work in a movie.

Some movies will be easier to use for evangelism than others, and it may take some creativity to intertwine the Gospel message with the movie's story. But rest assured that God is excited to reveal Himself to your friends who don't know Him yet. Just think – Jesus could be calling you and using you to reach people whom only *you* can reach, and maybe all you have to do is take them to the local movie megaplex this weekend!

Pray about It

- Pray that God will teach you how to be an effective witness and show you how to translate His love in a way people will understand.

Talk about It

- What do you think of the idea of Evangelist/Translator? Which part would be easier or harder for you? Why?

- Do you speak or act differently at church than you do at school or work? Do you find yourself saying or doing things that you wouldn't say or do with your church friends? If so, why did you act differently?

- Why did Jesus teach in parables? How is Talking Pictures similar to Jesus teaching in parables? Look through the Gospels and find a parable that you are less familiar with. Why are parables so powerful?

Live It Out

- This week, try to become aware of the times you find yourself separating the sacred and the secular in your life. Pay special attention to the occasions when you speak or act differently when you are home, at work, or out with friends than when you are at church. Note the circumstances and the people you were with, and think about why you chose to act differently at that moment.

- Have you ever made your own movies? Seeing how things work behind the scenes and creating with the movie audio/visual art form itself enhances one's understanding of the power of movies. It's a lot of fun to orchestrate the action and be involved in the creative process. Most computers come with basic movie-making/editing software. Give it a try!

Talking Pictures Example #2

"I guess *Aliens in the Attic* was actually pretty good for a kid's movie," Carson remarked as we drove home from the theater. Although we hadn't planned to see this particular movie, we decided to give it a try after our first choice was sold out.

"Yeah, it was pretty clever," I added, "but somewhat predictable."

"Well, *of course*, Jake – " he said sarcastically, "who else but tweens could possibly beat the aliens and save the world?"

"But I liked how they did it. They were creative," I pointed out. "The kids beat the aliens by doing things they already knew how to do. They used their video game talents, paintball skills, and even their math abilities. That's kind of cool."

"Yeah, that's true. They didn't all of a sudden learn karate and beat them that way," Carson said, breaking into his best Bruce Lee imitation.

I smiled at him as we drove along. I tapped my fingers on the steering wheel, trying to think of an idea that would help me tie our movie discussion into the Bible. I gathered my courage and prayed that he would be receptive. I looked over at Carson, who was holding his hands in a martial arts pose and making strange noises. I figured I had better grab him quickly.

"Hey, dude," I interrupted. "Have you ever heard the David and Goliath story?"

"Sure, I guess." Carson put his hands down and looked over at me curiously. "What about it?"

"Well, we were talking about kids being able to beat the aliens. It seems kind of unlikely, right? But something similar happened with David. You see, nobody could defeat Goliath – this huge giant. He was terrorizing everyone. Finally this kid David steps up and says, 'I'll take him out!' And everyone is thinking, 'yeah, right!' But David is determined to do it. But the king wanted David to use the same weapons that everyone else used – a sword, spear, shield, suit of armor. But none of that stuff fit him, because he was just a little kid." I paused, hoping Carson was still listening. "But David had his own method. He went out and fought Goliath with just 5 stones and a sling shot."

"Wow, that's just crazy. He must have been really brave!" Carson replied.

"It was more than just bravery," I continued. "David had a power that Goliath didn't. He told Goliath outright that the battle was the Lord's, and the Lord will win. David was not only true to himself, but true to his God as well. And God didn't let him down!"

Carson looked thoughtful for a moment. "That's kind of cool," he remarked. "I've never heard the whole story about David and Goliath before." He turned toward me. "So that was all, like, true? I thought some of those Bible stories were sort of like fairy tales."

"Nope – they're absolutely true," I assured him. "There are no fairy tales in the Bible. God's Word is all true. There are a lot of really interesting stories in the Bible, and David and Goliath is just one of them."

"I don't know a lot of those stories, actually," Carson admitted.

I took a deep breath, and continued. "You should come check out my church sometime. We've got a great Bible study group that meets on Wednesday evenings. It's very casual. They have a way of taking the stories from the Bible and making them come alive. I always have fun and get a lot out of it. Why don't you come along next week? It starts at 7. We can grab some dinner before we go."

Lights!

The Power of Story

The Old Testament begins with light. God spoke the words, **"Let there be light,"** (Genesis 1:3) and it was created. Can you imagine the utter darkness before God illuminated the world? Light is an amazing invention! A few thousand years later, the New Testament also begins with light, but this light is The Light of the World, Jesus Christ, coming to earth. Light is the beginning of the story and the very heart of the story. The Bible is made up of 66 different books by many different authors, but to put it simply, the Bible is God's story. It is the story of God at work in the world, and the story of God – the Creator, Savior, and Comforter – working in and through everyday, ordinary people like you and me.

Can you imagine what it must be like to see light for the very first time? Perhaps it was like the scene at the end of *The Truman Show* where Jim Carrey's character, Truman, opens the studio door at the end of the "world" and sees light – real, natural, God-given light, not the fake stuff he'd lived with his whole life in the television studio. Multiply that experience by a gazillion and you'll get a glimpse of what it's like to encounter the real light of Jesus for the very first time!

Jesus states in John 9:5, **"While I am in the world, I am the light of the world."** Jesus then goes on to make a startling statement in Matthew 5:14 – **"You are the light of the world."** Jesus is saying that *we, too*, are called to be the light of the world – a light that no darkness can ever overcome. You and I are part of the story of God at work in the world.

Why have we been called to be God's light in the world? Jesus continues in Matthew 5:16, **"let your light shine before men, that they may see your good deeds and praise your Father in heaven."** Our story is all about giving glory to God. Just like the moon reflects the light of the sun, we reflect His light. We are made in the image of God and are a reflection of that image. His story is our story, and we have been called to share that story with the world.

We are the continuation of the story. Some have called God's people the Fifth Gospel (the Bible has four Gospels: Matthew, Mark, Luke, and John), or the 29th chapter of Acts (the book of Acts has 28 chapters). I like both of those ideas because they remind us that the story must go on. When I was a kid, I used to wonder if I would ever do anything important enough to be added to the Bible. Then I was surprised to learn that people like Martin Luther and Mother Teresa aren't even *in* the Bible! How could that be? The Biblical canon may be closed, but the story of God continues on in the world through you. You're crucial to the plot of God's story!

The most important part of any movie is the plot, or the storyline. Now, granted, some movie plots make more sense than others. (Did anyone really understand the plot of *Dude, Where's My Car?*) But there is always some sort of storyline running through a film. Everyone is interested in a good story. Stories teach us, move us, and amuse us. The power of a well-crafted story is made evident when people can easily relate to it. I have always believed that our culture's fascination with gossip leads back to our basic need for stories. The paparazzi make a living trailing celebrities because we want to know their story.

Some people not only want to know the story but they also want to be a *part* of it. When baseball player Barry Bonds broke Hank Aaron's all-time homerun record in 2007, the parking lot of the stadium and the surrounding areas were full of people who wanted to be there and to be a part of history. None of them had a ticket to get into the game, but that didn't matter – they still wanted to be a part of the story.

Stories have been told throughout human history. Whether they are shared through oral tradition, written down, acted out, depicted in paintings, broadcast on the radio, or dramatized on our television or movie screens, stories are vital to who we are as humans. Whenever I speak to groups, I always marvel at the number of heads that perk up the moment the phrase, "Let me tell you a story," is uttered. I come from a long line of storytellers. My grandfather told us all sorts of stories when we were young. He told us the tale of the "Three Little Pigs" in his native German, using a thick accent and larger-than-life hand gestures. My father would often tell us stories to pass the time and to help my siblings and I fall asleep. And now I use the power of story to entertain and connect with my two young daughters. In the Adam Sandler movie, *Bedtime Stories*, the tales that he tells become real. But if you think about it, any good storyteller can bring a story to life.

Your Name in Lights

Each person's life is a story, and we are all the star of the movie of our lives. But our story becomes even more powerful when it connects to Jesus' story! Jesus says in Acts 1:8, **"you will receive power when the Holy Spirit comes on you."** Our power is the power of Jesus, which lives inside us and works through us.

As Spiderman's mild-mannered alter ego, Peter Parker, is reminded by his wise, old Uncle Ben, "With great power comes great responsibility." What is our responsibility as children of God? Look no further than the words that Jesus spoke right before His ascension. This section is better known as the Great Commission. **"Therefore go and make**

disciples of all nations, baptizing them in the name of the Father and of the Son and of the Holy Spirit, and teaching them to obey everything I have commanded you. And surely I am with you always, to the very end of the age." (Matthew 28:19-20). The Church is called to evangelize, baptize, and teach. As believers, it is our collective privilege and responsibility, with the power of the Holy Spirit living within us, to go forth and proclaim the Word of God. We have been called to GO! As individuals, it is our responsibility to use the spiritual gifts God has given us to go out into the world, witnessing to our friends and everyone we come into contact with in our own unique way.

Notice the last line in Jesus' directive here: **"And surely I am with you always."** (Matthew 28:20) We're not called to go forth all alone. Jesus is always with us! I have always enjoyed coaching sports, and I like to watch movies with inspirational coaching examples. Whether it's the old brutal coach in *Varsity Blues*, the young dynamic coaches in *Remember the Titans* and *We Are Marshall,* or the loving, crying football coach in *Invincible*, these memorable leaders have one major limitation in common. They cannot play the game for their players. All they can do is inspire, motivate, or even threaten, and then send the players off with a pat on the butt saying, "Go get'em!" However, that's not what Jesus does when he sends us forth into the world. Not only does He inspire and motivate us, but He also plays the game right alongside us. He empowers us. He strengthens us. His presence alone allows us to maximize and realize our full potential. Jesus promises that He will be with us *always!* How comforting to know that Jesus will be right there beside us, every moment of our lives!

In the book of Acts, chapter 9, we read the account of St. Paul's conversion. Talk about a story! He was literally and figuratively "knocked off his donkey." God explains His plan to Ananias, the man God chose to restore Paul's eyesight. In verse 11, God tells him to **"Go...,"** but like so many of us, Ananias made excuses as to why he shouldn't go. He had heard some rumors. He was afraid for his life. These are some of the same excuses we make when we don't "go." After listening for awhile, God tells him more emphatically in verse 15 to **"GO!"** God had to get out the exclamation point for Ananias! And to be honest, God needs to get out the exclamation point for the rest of us all too many times as well. Going forth and witnessing to others doesn't always come naturally to us. Sometimes it will be inconvenient, difficult, scary, and frustrating. But it's what God calls us to do.

The first step in "Talking Pictures" is knowing the story of Jesus, and how it resonates with your story.

The story of Jesus is one of redemption, forgiveness, and freedom. It is the story of love: unconditional, ever-lasting, undeserved, and unexplainable love. St. John tells us exactly why the Bible was written: **"Jesus did many other miraculous signs in the presence of his disciples, which are not recorded in this book. But these are written that you may believe that Jesus is the Christ, the Son of God, and that by believing you may have life in his name."** (John 20:30-31) The story of Jesus is the story of life – a life lived perfectly, and a life freely given.

Jesus' story is a paradox: opposites coming together, life out of death. We receive life, thanks to His death on the cross. Our life in Christ is also a paradox because we are simultaneously saint and sinner. We are saved and forgiven, but we're not perfect. We're still going to mess up every day of our lives. The connecting of our story to Jesus' story is done by the Holy Spirit. As Jesus Himself reminds us in Acts, chapter 1, we will receive power when the Holy Spirit connects us to Him! Before Jesus sends the apostles out with power to Jerusalem, Judea, Samaria, and the ends of the earth, He instructs them to wait in Jerusalem until they are baptized with the Holy Spirit. They are commanded to wait together, learning and growing, until they receive the power of the Holy Spirit. Now, for me, waiting is really frustrating. I prefer to just go. But waiting is often necessary to begin something that is worthwhile. We need to be connected with the Holy Spirit, our spiritual source, before we go forth as witnesses.

Once we understand how our own story is linked to God's plan of love and salvation for us in Christ, the wall that divided the secular and the sacred starts to crumble and fall. Our story becomes sacred but at the same time can act as a bridge to the secular, "real world" stories of others. Talking Pictures is a way to make this connection.

The Matrix movies ask so many powerful questions. What is the matrix? Is it real? What is worth fighting for? Can I trust my senses? Whom can I trust? Is ignorance better than reality? Am I special? Could I be the one to fulfill the prophecy? The first movie captured the imagination of its audience so powerfully because it asked so many intriguing questions. This movie allowed us to live inside the mystery, and didn't really give us any answers. But when the answers came in the two movie sequels, they didn't satisfy. In *The Matrix: Revolutions*, Agent Smith summed up the whole experience with the line, "The purpose of life is to end." What a horrible ending to a movie! It's no wonder that such an answer doesn't satisfy – it's far from the truth! As Christians, we know that this life is only the beginning! It's the beginning of the dream that God has had for you and me, and all of humanity, since the beginning of creation. This is the dream that was started in the Garden of Eden where God and man walked and talked together. And it's the dream of human perfection that will one day be fully realized in the Kingdom of Heaven. What a calling we have, to help others see God's dream and His incredible, life-changing love for us!

The story of Jesus is the most important story we will ever share. In the next chapter, we will examine the importance of relationships – both in the movies we watch as well as in our personal lives – and take a closer look at how our stories connect with one another through our relationship with Jesus.

Pray about It

- Pray that God will enable you to appreciate Jesus' story more fully and how it connects to your story.

Talk about It

- Think about the story of your life. What are some of your story's "highlights?" What are some of your life's defining moments?

- Have you seen Jesus at work in the difficult parts of your story? How?

- Do your friends know you're a Christian? How do they know for sure?

- Jesus tells us in Matthew 5:14, **"You are the light of the world."** In what ways does your light shine brightly for Jesus? In what areas is it a bit dim, i.e., where could you improve (with God's guidance)?

Live It Out

- Read the Gospel of Mark. It's the shortest of the four Gospels and is very fast paced. It's only sixteen chapters long. Often in our study of the Bible, we jump around in Scripture, reading a verse here and a verse there. You will be blessed to read the story of Jesus straight through. You will experience Jesus' story in a whole new way.

- What are some excuses you've used for why you think you can't go forth and share Jesus with others? Write down your reasons and pray about then. Ask God to help you overcome your fears and hesitations.

Talking Pictures Example #3

The snacks, drinks, and buddies were ready for what promised to be the greatest Saturday ever. "I've always wanted to spend a whole day watching all three *Matrix* movies in a row!" exclaimed my friend Ben, plopping himself down on the couch and ripping open a bag of chips. I had invited him over for the movie marathon, and I hoped that during the course of the day I'd find a good opportunity to share the Gospel message with him.

"Yeah, but what *is* the Matrix, exactly?" I tossed out the question, knowing it would get a discussion started.

"You still don't know, Grasshopper?" he replied in an accent reminiscent of the *Kung Fu* television series.

"Hey, you know I've never actually seen these movies," I reminded him. "I just quote from them because everyone does." I handed him a cold soda from the refrigerator and settled back into my chair.

"That's right... you've never seen any of these before!" Ben's eyes lit up with the anticipation of sharing his vast accumulation of *Matrix*-knowledge with me. The only thing Ben loved more than *The Matrix* movies themselves was talking about them to anyone who would listen.

"Okay, let me give you a little synopsis that will open your eyes to some of the trilogy's intricacies while never spoiling the plot." He rubbed his hands together excitedly and continued. "They *think* it's 1999, but it's really 2199, and nothing is real. The world as we know it all happens in our minds that are connected to a giant supercomputer that is using human beings as batteries. Neo is the one the oracle foretold would bring down the Matrix and set his people free. Trinity, Morpheus, and the rest of the gang are helping him do it." Ben bit into a chip, pleased with his summary.

I smiled at Ben's enthusiasm. "Hey, believe it or not, before you came over for this movie marathon, I did a little googling on *The Matrix* to get caught up. And I have to admit that this idea of a reluctant leader/savior is intriguing to me."

"Okay, Mr. Google, why is that?" he laughed, grabbing another handful of chips.

I had done my homework, and I knew this comment would give me an opportunity to bring the movie's story around to the Bible. "Well, if you think about it, many great leaders were reluctant at first. One that comes to mind is this guy named Moses."

"Moses? Oh yeah, Moses," Ben interrupted. "I heard of him before. What did he do again? Didn't he hold up a stick and divide the Red Sea or something?"

"Yeah, that's the guy," I continued. "But he did a lot more than that. He was called to be the leader of his people, the Israelites, and to free them from slavery in Egypt, which at the time controlled the world. Moses was the perfect man for the job. In fact, now I'll give *you* a little synopsis that will open your eyes to the story's intricacies," I smiled, paraphrasing his previous introduction. "However, unlike you, I may be spoiling the plot. Moses was the perfect man for the job because he lived in both worlds. Similar to Neo, actually! Moses was raised by the Egyptians and knew all there was to know about Egyptian culture. But he was by birth an Israelite. He was familiar with their culture and customs as well. So, when a leader was needed to free the slaves, he was the right man for the job. But you know what? He didn't want it! It seemed way too difficult. He was worried about what he *couldn't* do – not what he could do. But he was called by God to be the leader. He was the 'chosen one,' so he reluctantly did it."

"Did what?" Ben asked. "You didn't ruin the plot for me yet."

"He freed his people from slavery," I explained. "He performed miraculous signs and wonders, just like Neo, and by God's grace his people were given a whole new reality. In fact, that's also why Jesus came – to give His people a whole new reality. To set them free, so they would no longer be used and abused by the world."

"Hmm." Ben opened his can of soda. I sensed that he wasn't sure what to say next. Rather than risk pushing it and losing his interest altogether, I decided to save the rest of the discussion for later. I knew I'd have plenty of opportunities to point out more of the story parallels as we watched the movies all afternoon.

Breaking the silence, I said, "Man, if we don't start this trilogy now, we're not going to have time to watch all three! Let's start the movie!"

Camera!

The Power of Relationships

We need other people, especially when it's picture time. Sure, a photo by yourself is fine – but a picture with friends is so much more fun. Have you ever noticed how readily we ask complete strangers to hold our expensive cameras because we really want all of our friends and family to be in our photos? Relationships are worth so much more than expensive, but replaceable, cameras. If there's ever a fire in your house, you're going to grab the pictures, not the camera.

God greatly values relationships. Never forget that our faith life is about a relationship, not about rules or regulations – or even guidelines like the "Pirate's Code" in *The Pirates of the Caribbean: The Curse of the Black Pearl*. The Pirate's Code states that any man who falls behind is left behind. It's a good thing that Jesus doesn't work that way! Our relationship with Jesus should have a strong, positive effect on every other relationship we have. Certain Christian factions throughout the centuries have tried to make spirituality about following the "rules of the club." Many religious groups have tried to make faith life into an institution. But a relationship with Jesus is so much more!

I love to watch elderly couples, who have probably been married longer than I've been alive, walking hand in hand down the sidewalk. They have a genuine, long-lasting relationship. They have literally grown old together. In high school, if a couple has been together for a year, that's considered a really long time. But that's nothing compared to my grandparents, who've been married almost 60 years!

In Genesis, right after creating the very first member of the human race, God stated, **"It is not good for the man to be alone."** (Genesis 2:18) God is not just referring to romantic relationships here. He's talking about friendship, companionship, and community. We were created to be in relationships with other human beings. I believe the reason God created man first, and not man and woman together, was to show us how lonely life would be without relationships. God was teaching us from the very beginning that we need each other.

Having the companionship of family and friends isn't just an option in life. It's a necessary part of the human experience. Despite what Tom Hanks taught us in *Cast Away*, a volleyball is not an acceptable companion – even if it has a name and a blood splotch that kind of looks like a face. And while a dog may be considered man's best friend, dogs are not a substitute for human companionship, as Will Smith's character discovered in *I Am Legend*. He spent much of his time every day reaching out and looking for other human beings. Robots are also not an adequate substitute for human interaction and companionship, regardless of how human-like they are programmed to be, as in the movies *I, Robot; Lost in Space;* or *Artificial Intelligence: AI.* Even Data, the android in *Star Trek: The Next Generation,* longed to be human and to connect with human beings. Why? Because to be human is to interact with others. We need each other. We need human companionship.

King Solomon is known as being the wisest person in history. (If you're curious as to how he became so wise, read his backstory in 1 Kings chapter 3.) Solomon's writing in the Bible frequently mentions companionship, friendship, and community. In Ecclesiastes 4:10-12, he says this, **"If one falls down, his friend can help him up. But pity the man who falls and has no one to help him up! Also, if two lie down together, they will keep warm. But how can one**

keep warm alone? Though one may be overpowered, two can defend themselves. A cord of three strands is not quickly broken." Why do we need friendships? Quite literally – to keep us from breaking! They give us the necessary support that we cannot get any other way. Hoot, one of the soldiers in *Black Hawk Down*, explained in very simple terms why he fought: "It's about the man next to you, and that's it. That's all it is." Those in the military realize how much they trust and rely upon each other as a team, and how much stronger they are when they fight together. As brothers and sisters in Christ, we have the same need for reliance upon one another for strength and encouragement.

A common concern in the lives of many teenagers is the fear of not having many friends. High school can be a time of incredible loneliness. Many high schools contain thousands of students, and some even number higher than the population of many small towns. Yet it can be very easy for someone to get lost in the crowd, and feel lonely and isolated. There are so many teen movies that deal with these emotions. In the movie *The New Guy*, a student who's new to the school lies, cheats, and does anything he can think of to be noticed. Nobody goes to school thinking, "I want to be a mean girl." They become a "mean girl" in an attempt to fit in to a group. The need for acceptance is such a common and universal theme, and it points back to our basic need for meaningful relationships.

If you know someone who seems lonely, I encourage you to reach out to them. How can you befriend them? You don't have to become best friends, but you can show them kindness in your words and actions, and simply let them know that someone cares. When I was a kid, my dad always taught me that I should try to be friends with everyone. I now tell my daughters the exact same thing. It really doesn't take too much extra effort to be friendly and kind to others, and yet your thoughtful gesture or comment might mean so much in someone's life.

But what about those certain people we know who aren't very loveable? (I'm sure you know a few folks in that category!) Do we still have to show them kindness and love? Why should we bother? Because Jesus did! Jesus was frequently reaching out and befriending people who were shunned in their communities. Perhaps there is no better way to be like Jesus than to love those whom no one else wants to love. I've always been fascinated by the Zacchaeus story found in Luke 19:1-10. For some reason he's always been a character that has stuck in my mind. It's interesting that we only hear of Zacchaeus this one time in all of Scripture. Every Sunday School student knows that Zacchaeus was a "wee little man," (I've always pictured him being played by Danny DeVito!) and that Jesus invited Himself over to Zacchaeus's house. But did you know that Zacchaeus was despised and hated by everyone in his community? Because he was a tax collector, he was considered an outcast. Tax collectors were viewed as traitors because they were working for the dreaded Roman authorities. They also were usually "on the take," lining their own pockets with other people's money. To say that Zacchaeus wasn't very lovable is an understatement!

By the way, Zacchaeus wasn't just any tax collector. The Bible tells us that he was a *chief* tax collector. This is the only time this title is used in all of Scripture. Everyone hated Zacchaeus! He was on everyone's "most despised list." He was worse than Bill Murray in *Scrooged*. And yet Jesus befriended him, forgave him, and challenged him to change. Jesus welcomed him back into the family, and even told him that he is a **"son of Abraham"**! (Luke 19:9) Then in verse 10, Jesus gives us a perfect and simple explanation of His purpose: **"to seek and to save what was lost."** As followers of Jesus, this is our mission and purpose too. We are to love the unlovable, be a friend to the friendless, and do our best to ensure that the whole world knows that salvation is found in no one else but Jesus Christ (Acts 4:12). We can't kick back on the sofa and wait for the lost to come to us. We should be out there seeking... and finding.

God wants you to have many loving, meaningful relationships in your life. If you feel as though you are lacking in this area, I encourage you to make an extra effort to befriend someone else. The best way to find a friend is to reach out and be one to someone else. Most importantly, pray about the situation. You are an E.T., after all – you need to be phoning home! Never forget the power of prayer. There will be much more about prayer in later chapters. But for now, pray that God will put good, healthy friendships into your life. Like a good movie, life is a lot more fun and rewarding if you have good friends alongside you to experience it.

While friends and family are vital, the most important relationship that we need in our lives, hands down, is our spiritual relationship with Jesus. This is the relationship that all others are based on. As humans, we NEED God. We will never be spiritually whole without Him. For the unbeliever, there will always be something missing, something unfulfilled during his or her time on earth – and the void will be unbearable in the afterlife.

The Con-Flick

Almost every movie contains a conflict as part of its storyline. There is usually a good guy to cheer for and a bad guy to root against. And sometimes, as in *Ocean's Eleven*, the bad guy is even set up as the one that we cheer for. But in a good story, some degree of conflict is always present.

Conflict is a reality of life. General Patton is quoted in the movie *Patton* as saying: "Americans traditionally love to fight!" At one time or another, every single one of us has fought with someone else – our siblings, parents, spouse, children, friends, coworkers, etc. While we usually don't enjoy strife and arguments when they happen to us, we all love to watch other people's conflicts. Sports are an organized form of conflict. Soap operas are scripted conflict. Reality TV shows are set up to produce conflict. Maybe the reason we like to watch so much contention is that we are hoping to find the answers to our own conflicts. We're ultimately looking for redemption and the peace that passes all understanding.

We tend to think of peace as the absence of war. But as the Scriptures tell us, we will always have wars and rumors of wars (Matthew 24:6). Perhaps the key to peace in the mist of war is to take the words of St. Paul seriously in Romans, chapter 5, when he says, **"since we have been justified through faith, we have peace with God through our Lord Jesus Christ."** (Romans 5:1) Faith gives us the peace we need in our relationships when things get difficult. It doesn't make everything perfect, but it gives us the comfort and assurance of God's peace in our hearts in the heat of the battle.

In Matthew chapter 18, Jesus gives us some excellent advice on how to handle conflict in our relationships. He starts out in verse 15 with the phrase, **"If your brother sins against you…"** Note that He starts out His conflict resolution lecture with "if." *If* your brother sins against you. Not *when*, but *if*. That difference is actually very significant. It shows us the dream Jesus has for our Christian community. Communities belonging to the world will be full of conflict, sinfulness, and wars. But the communities of Jesus will be different. There will be unconditional, everlasting, unexplainable love. There will be people treating each other with respect, honor, and forgiveness.

It would be a huge mistake not to mention the reality of spiritual warfare in this section on conflict. As you live your life for Jesus, and as you are Talking Pictures, Satan is going to do whatever he can to stop you. He's going to try to discourage you and defeat you. Satan doesn't want you to share the grace and love of God with other people. But if there was ever a battle worth fighting, this is it! Ephesians 6:11 tells us, **"Put on the full armor of God so that you can take your stand against the devil's schemes."** Trust that God will use you to help make a difference in someone's eternal life.

In the movie *The Blind Side*, Michael Oher is a young man who, as a baby, lost his father. He grew up with a mother who was a drug addict. He experienced nothing good in his life until the age of 16 when, homeless, he was adopted. He was gifted with a very large and strong body, and learned how to use his gifts in football. But nothing really clicked for him and inspired him in football until he was told that his responsibility on the football team was to guard his family – the quarterback and running back – from the "enemy." Instantly his protective instincts took over and he stopped at nothing to guard his teammates. God wants us to have that kind of loyalty and concern for one another – our brothers and sisters in this world. As we deal with conflict in our relationships, let us never become so distracted and caught up in the problems that we lose sight of the prize that is ours in Christ Jesus. And let's share that great reward with everyone we come into contact with.

Contents Under Pressure

There is great power in relationships. There's potential for both the good and the not-so-good. Consider the double-edged sword of peer pressure. In the movie *Charlie Bartlett*, Charlie's key moment of self-realization comes during a conversation with his principal on the subject of popularity. In a heated exchange, the principal reminds him that there are more important things than popularity, and Charlie argues, "Like what? 'Cause I'm 17. And right now popularity's pretty important!" Without skipping a beat, the principal responds, "Like what you *do* with that popularity." Charlie's interaction with his fellow students, who literally worship the ground he walks on, changes dramatically after this realization. He decided there and then to use the influence of his popularity for good!

You don't have to look very far to see the negative effects of peer pressure in movies. It can be found in just about every movie ever made about teenagers. *American Pie, Varsity Blues, Mean Girls, Can't Buy Me Love...* even the beloved Troy fell to peer pressure in all three of the *High School Musical* movies! It's a significant reality of life, and not just for teenagers. Children start becoming sensitive to the persuasion of their peers as early as preschool. Adults struggle with peer pressure at work and in social groups – they just don't have the mandatory assemblies in the school gymnasium to address it. But as I mentioned earlier, peer pressure can work both ways. While it tends to have a negative connotation, peer pressure can also be a tool for positive change. I have seen it influence people to do incredible good: go on mission trips, pursue a career in ministry, change destructive behaviors, and reach great pinnacles of success. But far too often, we see the destructive side of negative peer pressure and its result – the stuff that destroys families and marriages, devastates careers, shreds friendships, and ruins lives through drugs and other under-mining behaviors.

Speaking of the evils of peer pressure, do you need to get rid of some of your friends? I know that may sound harsh, but you've probably heard the expression, "you are who you roll with." Over the years, I have met many people who have made radical changes in their lives to overcome addictions, or to remove themselves from harmful influences. They all admitted that in order to truly change, they had to get rid of some of the people they associated with who were encouraging or enabling these destructive behaviors. Your friends speak volumes about who you are. What does your choice of friends say about *you*?

The people who will be the most open and receptive to what we have to say about Jesus are those who are the closest to us and with whom we share a true relationship. We have to earn the right to be heard. Theodore Roosevelt once said, "People don't care how much you know until they know how much you care." This is so true, and worth remembering. In the Robin Williams movie, *Patch Adams*, his character says, "I love you without knowing how, why or even from where." But the blessing for Christians is that we *do* know where our love comes from! **"We love because he first loved us."** (1 John 4:19) We will be much more effective in reaching people in Jesus' name through our kindness and love than through any amount of preaching we may do. The trust and respect we have earned from those closest to us will open doors for us that would remain closed to others.

Too often we have the mental image of an evangelist as the crazy guy on the street corner with a bullhorn. In the movie *2012*, which portrays the end of the world as we know it, there is a funny line from one of the politicians who has just learned of the coming disaster: "Kind of galling when you realize that nutbags with cardboard signs had it right the whole time." Or perhaps when we think of evangelists, we picture the angry protesters outside the Marilyn Manson concert waving boycotting signs, or the zealots shoving flyers into our hands that explain the intricate details of hell and how we're going to burn for all eternity. Or maybe we think of the groups promoting a website filled with horrible pictures of fetuses mutilated from abortions. While these shock tactics may be considered one way to evangelize, those folks have not *earned* the right to be heard by their audience. You have earned the right to be heard by your friends because they respect you and value who you are.

While the first step in Talking Pictures is knowing Jesus' story and how it's unfolding in your story, the second step is recognizing those who Jesus has put into your life and do not yet know Him as Lord and Savior.

Have you ever thought about the fact that God may have placed people in your life for the sole purpose of your reaching out to them with the story of Jesus? Just possibly, you may be the only chance that someone may ever have to hear the Gospel message! That idea sends shivers up my spine. That's a huge responsibility AND a tremendous opportunity. I don't believe in coincidences – do you? As V said in *V for Vendetta*, "There are no coincidences, Delia... only the illusion of coincidence." Every single person you encounter could be a divine appointment arranged by God Himself. God's going to accomplish His work, and He wants to use you! Maybe it's time to re-focus the lens and see who God has put into your life for a greater purpose: friends, family members, acquaintances, coworkers, classmates, club members, teammates, roommates, etc. Grab the camera, and explore the possibilities!

Pray about It

- Pray for God to reveal specific people He has placed in your life for you to share your story (and His story) with.

Talk about It

- What are the most important relationships in your life? Why are they so precious to you?

- Is conflict inevitable in relationships? Why or why not?

- Why is it so hard to resist peer pressure? What are some things we can do when we feel pressured to "go along with the crowd?"

- Can you think of a recent example when peer pressure has had a negative impact or damaging effect in your life? Can you think of an example when peer pressure had a positive effect on you?

Live It Out

- Think of a few people whom you've found to be difficult and even "unlovable." Resolve to reach out to these people in love and forgiveness, trusting in the power of the Holy Spirit. Remember that Jesus sought out and befriended those whom no one else wanted to love. Pray for these individuals regularly, even though initially you may find this challenging. Prayer changes things. Pray that God will use YOU to help bring about positive change in each of your lives.

Talking Pictures Example #4

As we walked out of the theater, my friend exclaimed, "Man! That was an excellent movie! And to think I was a little hesitant to see *District 9* because I hadn't seen Districts 1 through 8..."

"Seriously, Adam –" I rolled my eyes at him, "that joke wasn't funny when you said it about *Apollo 13, Ocean's Eleven*, or even *Fantastic Four!*"

Adam laughed at his own joke, and then grew serious. "You know, it's not every day that an action movie makes you think."

"And it's not every day that you *think!*" I teased.

Ignoring my comment, he continued. "Seriously, though. Think about all the brutality in the world. People abusing or mistreating people because of their skin color or gender – only allowing them to live in certain areas because of their background."

I sensed that I might be able to go deeper with this conversation, so I said a silent prayer and ventured out on a limb. "Have you ever heard the story of the Good Samaritan?"

Adam squinted for a moment. "I don't think so," he said. "Why?"

We crossed the street and walked toward the parking garage. "Well, the story goes that one day, a man was walking along the road when some thugs jumped out, beat him up and robbed him. Then they left him on the side of the road. Well, several people passed by on the road and saw him lying there. But nobody wanted to stop and help him. And – "

"Sounds like New York City!" Adam interrupted. "People see stuff happen and they don't want to get involved. That's awful."

"And what's worse, the people who passed by were people you would've thought would stop to help – priests and stuff. But they didn't. And this guy was badly hurt, and wouldn't survive if he didn't get medical attention." I paused the story as we climbed the stairs to the level where my car was parked.

"So what happened to him?" Adam asked impatiently, knowing my tendency to draw out a story for dramatic effect. I smiled to myself.

"Okay, so along comes this guy down the road, and he's a Samaritan. Now, a Samaritan was an outcast. They were people who were treated badly and forced to live in certain areas – kind of like in the movie we just saw. Nobody wanted anything to do with them. But guess what? The Samaritan actually stopped when he saw the injured man. He felt sorry for him and wanted to help him. He bandaged him up, put the poor guy on his own donkey and took him to a doctor. And the Samaritan even paid the hospital bills! A Samaritan was the last person that anyone would have thought would stop and do such a kind thing." I fished my keys out of my pocket and unlocked the car. "The story reminds us that our differences aren't important. What is important is love and helping those in need."

"Where's that story from?" Adam asked, sliding into the passenger seat. "Did you say the Bible? I remember that some of your other stories have come from there."

"Yes, you're right," I replied. "In fact, it was one of the stories that Jesus taught." I turned and reached into the back seat to grab my well-worn Bible. I opened it up to Luke chapter 10 and handed it to him. "There's a lot more stories in here that you might find interesting as well…"

Action!

The Power of Movies

If a picture is worth a thousand words, what are movies worth? At 24 frames per second, a 2-hour movie contains 172,800 pictures. At a rate of 1,000 words per picture, that adds up to 172,800,000 words! With that many words at stake, it is time to start Talking Pictures!

In their most basic form, movies are simply still frame pictures set in motion. These fast-moving pictures trick the eye into thinking there is a fluid, seamless image. But movies contain so much more than a series of pictures sequenced together. Movies have power! They have the power to entertain, teach, and inspire. They can introduce bold new ideas and trends – some positive, some negative – into our culture. They can frighten us or enlighten us. They can make us laugh until we cry, or cry until we laugh. Movies connect us with the world around us, help us relate to others, and sometimes even give us a better understanding of ourselves. Movies have power, and we can use this power to help us share our faith in Jesus.

In the first chapter of John's Gospel, we are reminded that Jesus is the Word of God. He is the Word made flesh; He is the Word in action. He doesn't just speak the Gospel – He *is* the Gospel! God came to earth in Jesus, lived the perfect life that we never could, and died the brutal death that we would never want to experience. He bore the sins of the world on His back, and rose from the dead under His own power. That's larger-than-life action. That's *love* in action!

God calls us to grow in our faith, and to be people of action. St. James expresses this powerfully: **"faith by itself, if it is not accompanied by action, is dead."** (James 2:17) Not "mostly dead," like the Dread Pirate Roberts in *The Princess Bride*. Faith without works IS dead! However, a dead faith can come back to life when, by the power of the Holy Spirit, that life is given away and focused on the needs of others. Faith with works of selfless service is a growing, living faith. In the words of Dr. Frankenstein, "IT'S ALIVE!" And as Jesus proved, even the gates of hell will not be able to stop it!

"Picking up our cross" is a phrase that Jesus uses not once but twice in both the Gospels of Matthew and Luke. What does this mean? Many people assume it's about bearing our burdens, but Jesus tells us to cast our burdens onto Him (1 Peter 5:7). It's also not about merely surviving this life and looking forward to heaven. Yes, heaven is greater than anything we can imagine, but Jesus wants us to be joyful and thrive in this life as well (John 15:11). Picking up our cross is about giving ourselves away. It's about living our lives for others in selfless service. It's about following Jesus. This was His first and last command to His disciples, and it is His command to us as well. Life is meaningful only when it is lived for others.

The funny thing about life is that you get so much more out of it by giving it away. Maybe this is why so many people wrestle with what life is all about. The meaning of life is a widely universal theme in movies, because we all want to know why we were put on this earth. What is our purpose? Why are we here right now – in this place and time? What a shame that Curly died in *City Slickers* before he could tell us the one thing that life was all about!

In the movie *Slumdog Millionaire*, we see the story unfold of a young man in the slums in India who has experienced a difficult and painful upbringing. He is a contestant on the Indian version of the television game show,

Who Wants to Be a Millionaire? With every question he gets right, we see flashbacks of how he experienced the particular questions and answers in real life. The character tells a detective who accuses him of cheating that he wishes he *didn't* know the answers, because great suffering had to be endured to learn those realities. But he needed to go through that to win the millions and realize the ultimate prize of his one true love. Life can be confusing and difficult at times, but we often gain a little insight and perspective as we watch a movie's story.

Many movies try to present an understanding of the big picture of life. As Ian, the genius chaos theory expert in *Jurassic Park*, says, "Life finds a way." And since we know that Jesus is The Life, we also know that He will find a way to lead us to Him, and enable us to learn the *true* meaning of life. Many movies contain themes that revolve around a journey or quest for something important to the main character. *Dumb and Dumber*, *Titanic*, and *Finding Nemo* are just a few examples. Although the heroes all have their own difficulties and challenges – they may not be very bright, they may have a little fin, they may be poor or trapped in a loveless relationship – they always find a way to make it through the journey. The journey is never easy; if it was, it wouldn't make such a good story! Our life's journey won't always be easy or smooth, but remember that Jesus will always be there every step of the way

We think of movies as being larger than life. Movies are an art form that uniquely captures the imagination and stimulates the senses of sight and sound. Have you ever listened to the director or actor commentary on a DVD? Nearly every DVD or Blu-ray disc released today contains some kind of commentary. When this concept first came out, many people feared that it would ruin the movie magic. However, I feel that it enhances the overall enjoyment of the movie. In the commentaries, we learn how different scenes were composed and shot, and why the directors and actors made certain decisions. Throughout the entire film, every single frame is planned out in excruciating detail. This isn't to say that mistakes aren't made in the production of movies. Even the world's finest filmmakers allow mistakes to slip into the final cut. The Internet Movie Database (www.imdb.com) actually has a link under each movie title called "Goofs" where users can submit and share mistakes they have found in the movie. Some of the goofs are as insignificant as a jacket being zipped up from one camera angle and then unzipped from another. But some mistakes are much bigger, such as the actor being referred to by his real name as opposed to the character's name. Painstaking efforts go into every phase of the movie-making process to produce a flawless film, but every movie still contains some goofs. As in life, mistakes happen. Movie action is full of details, large and small, and they are all very carefully created.

The Reel World

Movies are really nothing more than visual story-telling. The quality of the story is the key to the movie-making business. The better the overall story, the better the movie's potential. Have you ever gotten into one of those arguments about which is better – the book or the movie? If so, you know that most people usually feel that the book is better. Why? The written word can take a good story and combine it with our own imaginations to become something even more powerful. A movie version has to capture both of those elements – story and imagination – and create them for us. To do this well is extremely difficult, which is why those few films that *do* succeed often become blockbusters.

Movies have the potential to melt away fears, and the power to create new ones. Fear of sharks skyrocketed after the release of *Jaws*. My wife lived in Hawaii as a child, and refused to go in the ocean for years due to a *Jaws*-inspired terror of the great man-eating shark. UFO-related sightings (and hysteria) increased dramatically after the release of *Independence Day*. Of course we know that if there *is* intelligent life out there, they will be wise enough to attack earth right after a big Hollywood blockbuster shows us how to defeat them! Interestingly enough, Will Smith sightings also increased dramatically after the release of *Independence Day*. I am proud to admit that I actually own several Fresh Prince cassette tapes. (If you are too young to know what a cassette tape is, ask your parents!)

Movies, at their heart, are stories that can connect and unite – however, not always in a healthy way. More than a few movies gave me nightmares as a kid. I still can't watch *The Exorcist* to this day. Even seeing a commercial for the movie brings back that feeling of terror that I felt as a child when I watched it at a friend's house (against the better judgment of my parents, who warned me not to see it). It left a mark on me that still haunts me after all these years. Now that I am a parent myself, I try to use good judgment in deciding which movies I will allow my children to watch. Movies have the power to affect us deeply, but sometimes in a very negative way.

At the heart of who we are as Christians is a story, too. It is a story that is filled with the themes of betrayal, love, sadness, joy, forgiveness, redemption, and salvation. Hollywood has been exploring these topics in major motion pictures since the beginning of the movie business. These themes work because everyone has experienced many, if not all of them, in one way or another. They are meaningful and compelling, and they are part of our own personal stories. In the movie *Australia*, Hugh Jackman reminds us, "All a man really owns is his story." Our story is ours, and ours alone.

Movies have the power to communicate a story differently than any other medium. Movies aren't interrupted by commercials – or, at least, they weren't originally intended to be. Have you ever watched a movie on network television and been frustrated by all the commercial breaks? The suspense in the movie builds to a feverish pitch and we are on the edge of our seats waiting for the aliens to attack, and suddenly we are watching an ad for dog food or furniture polish. Commercials disrupt the flow and continuity of the story. This was not the intention of the filmmakers. In fact, movie theaters are becoming more strict with people who distract from the movie experience with crying babies, cell phone calls, and text messages. The goal of a movie experience is an uninterrupted story. Even the simplest of stories can be used to communicate very complicated concepts. It is nearly impossible to deny the power of a good, well-told, and constructed story.

Despite all of the best filmmaking efforts, 3-D technology, storytelling techniques, high tech special effects, and perhaps even a famous cast of actors, a story is meaningful because of the way people *connect* to it. As Christians, our call is not to simply tell The Story, but to *live* it! The Story, of course, is of God's love for us – a love so great that He sent His one and only Son into the world to live the perfect life that we cannot. That love caused God to come to us in human form (Jesus) and experience everything that we experience, except He never sinned. Sinful people put Him to death, but His love was so great that death did not triumph. Three days later He rose from the dead. He has won the victory for us. Today He lives within us, and works through us to change the world! Jesus loves the world and wants to use you to bring His story alive for everyone you meet.

Let's summarize what we've learned: *The first step in Talking Pictures is knowing the story of Jesus and how it ties into your story. The second step is recognizing that Jesus has put people into your life who do not yet know Him as Lord and Savior. The third step is seeing Jesus' and your story unfolding in the film, and being able to share this with your friends.*

As I mentioned previously, the goal of this book is to teach and encourage people to use movies as a way to initiate conversations with others about the grace given to us through Jesus. You can use the natural power of movies, and the fascination we have for them, to talk about your faith and the power and glory of God working in your life. As you get more and more into the ministry of Talking Pictures, it is my hope and prayer that you will never watch a movie in the same way again. I hope you start "translating" movies, and then move on to television, video games, magazines, the Internet, school, sports, and everything else that you once thought of as secular, and begin to see the omnipresent God at work in a sacred way. Before long, you won't just be Talking Pictures – you'll be "Talking Everything," and seeing God at work in ways you never imagined.

It's time to jump in. This is the fun part. Are you ready? Take your friend to a movie. Any movie will do. Consider letting them pick the movie, so later on it won't seem as though you were setting something up. Pray for God's guidance. Erase that line between the sacred and secular, and see how God is truly at work. As in most things in life, seeing God's hand at work will become easier with experience. Bill Murray's character in *Groundhog Day* had to practice over and over to get just one day of his life right, but eventually he figured it out. I have confidence that with a little practice, you'll get more comfortable with your new role as Evangelist/Translator!

The great thing about taking a friend to a movie as a method of witnessing is that if they don't quite get it, that's okay. There will be a whole new batch of movies coming out next week, next month, and so on. Maybe one of those will resonate better with them. Keep focusing on spiritual things, and you will find them where you least expect it. In the remaining chapters of this book, I am going to take a closer look at different ways in which you can see God at work in any movie. The first way is to look for relatable characters. Can you see yourself in any of the movie's characters? Or perhaps you recognize other people you know. These relatable characters can act as a mirror for your own thoughts and feelings (or those of your friend), and this can help you to express yourself and your faith in different ways.

The second way is to look for relatable situations. What situations in the movie have you experienced personally, on some level? How did you struggle through and overcome those challenges? Did you react the same way as the character in the movie? Why or why not? Relatable situations can open new doors to barrier-breaking conversations.

The final and perhaps most important way to see God at work is to look for redemptive themes. We all need to be saved from something. A very effective way to use movies to point to Jesus as our Savior and Redeemer is through redemptive themes that show forgiveness, freedom, and love. Jesus is the Savior of the world! There is nothing that He cannot overcome.

Like an innocent Andy Dufresne crawling through a tunnel of disgusting human waste to escape from prison in *The Shawshank Redemption*, we all have to endure difficulties to reach the point of freedom. We all desire the sweet freedom that Jesus brings! Jesus came that we may have life, and as He says in John 10:10, He wants us to have life to the FULL!

It's time... Lights, Camera, Action!

Pray about It

- Pray that by God's grace, you will continue to live your life for others in selfless service.

Talk about It

- Movies have the potential to melt away fears, and the power to create new ones. Can you think of a recent movie example of each?

- When was the last time you shared the story of Jesus with someone who has never heard it?

- What are some of the miracles that God is working in your life? How can you share these blessings with your unchurched friends?

- What are some practical ways we can live our lives for others in selfless service?

Live It Out

- Plan to invite one of your non-Christian friends to a movie sometime this week. Consider your friend's personality as you choose the particular movie and venue. Would this person be more comfortable having a spiritual discussion at home as you watch a DVD together, or after going out to see a new release at the movie theater? Would it be easier to have the discussion one-on-one, or in a small group? Perhaps you can think of some mutual Christian friends whom you could enlist in the mission as well.

Talking Pictures Example #5

"Knowing is half the battle!" we shouted as we left the theater. My neighbor Mike and I had been looking forward to seeing this movie. As kids, we had both been huge G.I. Joe fans.

"I was wondering how they were going to work that classic G.I. Joe line into the movie," Mike commented. "But they actually did it pretty early on in the film, which is funny because in the Saturday morning cartoons it was always at the end."

"That's because knowing *is* half the battle. And if you know that in the beginning, it makes the battle a whole lot easier!" I pointed out.

"So what's the other half of the battle?" Mike asked.

"Well, I would say it's taking action," I replied. We walked outside into the bright afternoon sun and I reached for my sunglasses. "Knowing is great, but you still gotta act on it."

"What do you mean?"

"Well, people know all kinds of stuff," I explained, "but it doesn't do them any good if they fail to follow through on it. Think about the warnings we've heard a million times. 'Smoking is bad for you.' 'Don't eat too much junk food.' 'Don't drink and drive.' 'Brush only the teeth you want to keep.' But if we don't do anything with the knowledge, then knowing it is pointless. I mean, – "

"Wait!" Mike interrupted, teasingly. "You don't brush your teeth?"

"No, I do," I laughed. "You're missing my point. Just knowing something is not enough. It needs to be connected with *doing*." We headed across the theater parking lot to grab an early dinner at the new taco place.

"Okay, I get it," Mike said. "Yeah, everybody needs to do what they think is right."

"Well, it isn't so much about you and I doing whatever we think is right. It's more about getting our information from a reliable source. Just like in the *G.I. Joe* movie. The general gave the orders. The soldiers didn't just go off and do whatever they felt was right. They followed their leader because he knew what was best for them." We stopped to let a few cars go by and then kept walking. "It's the same for us," I continued. "We need to be sure we can really trust what we believe to be true."

"Well, okay," Mike interjected, "but how do we know the information we have is really true? Kind of like the whole weapons of mass destruction thing in Iraq. I mean, people sometimes base their whole lives and actions on stuff that someone might have said with authority. But what if it turns out to be false? Like the health experts who say 'Eat this – it's good for you,' and then a week later, 'Don't eat this – it will give you cancer.' Or scientists come up with some type of wonder drug and it turns out to have side effects that will kill you."

We took our place at the end of a rather lengthy line at the restaurant counter. I didn't mind the wait, knowing that it would give us time to keep talking. I could see that this conversation could easily be brought around to Jesus. "Good examples!" I continued, and repeated his question aloud. "How do we know that our information is trustworthy?"

"I don't know," Mike sighed. "How can you really trust anything or anyone?"

I had my open door. I paused to say a silent prayer, and then replied, "Well, for some things in life, like you

mentioned, all we can do is try to follow the recommen-
dations of experts and hope it is right. But for the things in
life that really matter – the deeper things – we do have a
reliable and accurate source. It's the Bible. It's God's Word,
and it is true and infallible. When we follow it, we know that
we're doing the right thing and making the right decisions."

Mike was quiet for a moment, and then spoke up.
"But there are lots of religions in the world. They can't ALL
be right." I knew that Mike had once mentioned that he
shunned religion as a whole because he was confused as to
which one had the true message. Rather than risk choosing
the wrong one, he had decided it was safer to avoid them all.

I prayed that the Holy Spirit would give me the
wisdom and the words I would need. "Jesus said, 'I am the
way, the truth and the life. No one comes to the Father except
through me.'"

"But anyone could make that claim," Mike interrupted. "Saying it doesn't mean that it's true. Can you prove
it?"

I smiled knowingly. "I don't have to prove it," I
replied, "because Jesus Himself proved it. He proved it by
allowing Himself to be the perfect sacrifice, dying the death
we ourselves deserved. He said He would rise again and have
victory over death and Satan, and He did. He promised, and
He followed through. If He's got power over death, then He
already knows what the whole battle is about!" I smiled at
Mike as the man behind the counter handed us our order on a
tray.

We took our food to a table and sat down. Mike bit
into his burrito, and looked at me curiously as I said a silent
prayer over my food before I started to eat.

"I don't know that much about Jesus and the Bible,"
Mike admitted. "Maybe it would make more sense to me if I
actually read it."

"Definitely," I readily agreed. "Learning more is a great idea. Knowledge is power." I smiled. "And knowing is half the battle, right?"

Mike laughed. "Okay, but what's the other half?"

"Faith," I told him. "Life still won't make sense all of the time, but faith is believing that God is in control even when it appears there's nothing but chaos. Faith is all about trusting in Jesus and His promises."

Mike looked thoughtful as he continued to eat. "I don't know if I can really believe it," he confessed, "but I think I'd like to hear more about it."

Take 1

Relatable Characters

In the next few chapters, we're going to explore the most common elements in movies that people can relate to and identify with. How would you define "relate?" Think of it as finding connections or similarities between two different things. It's kind of like being "related" to your family members. Most people love a good family comedy because we can identify with the joys and frustrations of these close relationships. We laugh at the embarrassment that Chevy Chase's character, Clark Griswold, faces in the classic *Vacation* movies whenever Cousin Eddie is around. Most of us have at least one wacky (or just plain weird) relative that we're not always proud of, but we know that they're still part of our family. Or perhaps we're forced to relate to new family members whom we just don't feel we have anything in common with, as in the movie *Step Brothers*. They don't listen to our rules, and they turn our lives completely upside down. Whether embarrassing or stressful, family relationships can be a curse or a blessing – and to be honest, they're usually a mix of both! Family relationships depicted in movies are often easy to relate to because we have such strong feelings about our own family relationships.

And this is just one example. Relating to a story element draws us deeper into the narrative, and once you're drawn into a story, you're more likely to be influenced by other elements of the story. Telling a friend how a certain story element has a parallel to your Christian faith can be a powerful witness. Find those connections – those relatable elements – and you'll be Talking Pictures like an experienced Evangelist/Translator before you know it.

We're All Characters

Think back to some of the very first movies you ever saw as a little kid. Remember how much fun it was to pretend you were a character in the movie? You really believed you were part of that movie yourself. You were Cinderella at the ball, meeting and dancing with the prince, all the while wondering if this was really love. You were Luke Skywalker or Princess Leia, using the Force, a lightsaber, and occasionally a blaster to fight and destroy the evil Empire. You were truly Harry Potter – scar, magic wand, book of magic spells and all. You were one of the Teenage Mutant Ninja Turtles, and you ate as much pizza as you possibly could to prove it. Perhaps you even looked like a hobbit.

As a child, I would spend hours pretending and playing the role of the hero in all of the adventures I saw in the movies. I believe that even as adults, we still enjoy finding ourselves in the adventures and misadventures of our favorite characters. Finding a character or two that we can relate to is a huge part of the overall moviegoing experience. We enjoy the movie more because we know that *could* be us… or maybe we wish that it *would* be us… or perhaps we think that it *should* be us, and need to wrestle with why it isn't. Maybe we simply thank God that the guy in the movie *isn't* us! Any way you look at it, we often can see ourselves wrapped in the characters in the movies we watch.

A good male friend of mine loves chick flicks, and he admits that the reason he likes them so much is because he always seems to find a relatable character – usually the one that is unlucky in love. He was really looking forward to seeing the movie, *He's Just Not That Into You*, with its large cast of famous people, including Ben Affleck and Jennifer Aniston. But he left the movie very disappointed. Although he felt that the movie itself was well-done, he was disillusioned because he couldn't relate to any of the characters.

Part of the phenomenon that surrounds the block-buster *Avatar* is that people are going into depression because the world of Pandora is so beautiful but not at all real. They long for a place like that. They wish they could be a part of the world of Avatar so much that it is actually ruining their "real" life. (Maybe some people are relating *too* much!)

There is something important about being able to identify with a character. It captures our imaginations and draws us into the movie. Movie producers invest a great deal of money on focus groups, asking random, ordinary people about the relatability of their characters. Once we see ourselves in the movie, we can compare our own thoughts, feelings and actions to those of the character. Would we have chosen that path? Would we have the guts to stand up to the unfair, brutal coach like the main character in *Mr. Woodcock*? Which side would we have chosen: that of the blue Na'vi in *Avatar,* or the greedy humans? Would you pick up the homeless teenager like Sandra Bullock did in *The Blind Side*? Life is full of choices and potential paths. Each one has different consequences. And yet we have the promise **"that in all things God works for the good of those who love him."** (Romans 8:28)

Because God gave us the gift of free will, we have the freedom to make all kinds of bad decisions. However, God also gives us the ability to make good choices. Instead of abusing God's gift of free will by going along with the popular tide, making a decision to do the right thing can be a powerful witness to our friends. This isn't because we're perfect people – we're as sinful as the next guy – but we are able to make good choices because of Jesus working within us! Perhaps the strongest witness we can make as Christians is to have our God-pleasing words and opinions line up with our actions. We should "walk the talk," as they say.

Now, I want to make myself clear. I am not a chick-flick guy, and thankfully my wife isn't a chick-flick chick either. But one such movie we saw together was *Fools Rush In*, with Matthew Perry and Salma Hayek. It's the story of a couple who fall in love, despite their vast differences – it's the whole "opposites attract" thing. But they meet at the most inconvenient time in both of their lives. They each were just starting to understand and enjoy single life, and weren't looking for a lifelong companion. But they found each other, nonetheless. In the movie, it seems as though everything these two characters try to do ends up backfiring. Their family and friends think they're crazy for even trying to make things work. Now, I know this sounds like the basic plot of every chick-flick ever made. But for whatever reason – perhaps it was a special time in our lives – my wife and I saw ourselves in this movie.

Let me just clarify that our situations weren't exactly the same as the characters in the film. In the movie, they get pregnant before marriage, while we didn't have children until after five years of marriage. The clash of cultures in the film is between Hispanic and New Yorker; for my wife and I, it's a difference in backgrounds (she's a military brat who grew up in Hawaii and Asia, and I'm a German Lutheran church-worker-brat, raised in the Midwest). Despite these differences, we could relate to the characters. We saw each other in the movie. We did enter each other's lives at a seemingly inconvenient time. But God certainly had a plan for us. We can't imagine life without each other now. The movie helped us to laugh at ourselves and our differences. In a surprising and unexpected way, this simple, mediocre romantic comedy actually helped strengthen our marriage, and our appreciation for one other.

I saw *Meet the Parents* after having been married for a few years, and it made me laugh as I recalled some of the awkward moments I had faced when trying to connect with my future in-laws. There were so many times when I feared I wasn't earning their respect and approval. Watching the movie's main character, Greg, tell his in-laws that he was going to be a nurse reminded me of the conversation I had with my future father-in-law when I informed him that I was going to become a poor, starving church-worker. Then, years later, as only God with His infinite sense of humor would have it, I actually watched the movie's sequel, *Meet the Fockers* with my father-in-law. Talk about relating to a movie! There were some hilarious scenes that I couldn't laugh at outwardly because they hit a little too close to home! But we did have some amusing conversations afterward.

As you watch a movie, try to put yourself into the shoes of various characters and see how the conversations with your companions unfold. You don't have to have a perfectly matched, point-for-point connection with a character to identify with him or her. You can learn something new about yourself by seeing yourself in the movie. Yes, the camera may add ten pounds – or ten problems you didn't know you had – but life is about learning and growing. Remember what *G.I. Joe* says: "Knowing is half the battle!" What's the other half? Maybe the other half is growing. First we know and understand God's love, as it is revealed to us in Scripture, and then by God's grace we grow into the person He has dreamed us to be. And as we continue to learn and grow in God's love, we will want to share those things with others who don't yet know Him.

Bible Characters Are People Too

The wisest person who ever lived – King Solomon – tells us in the book of Ecclesiastes that **"there is nothing new under the sun."** (chapter 1, verse 9) Now, as you ponder this statement, remember that King Solomon lived about 3,000 years ago. He never saw the space shuttle, the iPod, the Nintendo Wii™, plasma TV, or my personal choice for the greatest invention of all time: Velcro®. And yet he was still inspired by the Holy Spirit to write that there is nothing new under the sun! Nothing new? That idea could be limiting, or perhaps it's liberating.

Think about that from a temptation angle. Satan's the expert at what he does – he's the Devil, after all – but remember that he's only got so many tricks in his bag. His power is limited, especially in light of the unlimited power of our Heavenly Father. Satan is more powerful than you and I (as all of the angels are), but remember: **"the one who is in you is greater than the one who is in the world."** (1 John 4:4) You see, it isn't about you. It's about Jesus working *in* you and *through* you. Greater is He, and He has chosen to live inside of you! What a comforting and empowering thought that is!

Temptations may change their general appearance, but basically they are still the same old temptations through time. King David being tempted by a nude, rooftop-bathing Bathsheba (2 Samuel 11:2) isn't any different than us being tempted by Internet pornography. Lust is still lust. Noah being tempted with alcohol and drunkenness, right after spending what must have seemed like an eternity on the ark (Genesis 9:20-21), isn't any different than us being tempted to get drunk with our friends at a party. Substance abuse is still substance abuse. Judas being tempted by greed with thirty pieces of silver (Matthew 26:15) isn't any different than us being tempted to cheat on our income taxes, or illegally download music or movies from the Internet. Greed is still greed, whether it's greed for accumulating more money, or for saving money by not paying for something. Technology will keep changing, and human beings will continue to dream up new ways to get in trouble. But when we strip it down to its basic form, there really is no *new* temptation. We can take comfort in the fact that God has promised to help us overcome the temptations that we face in our lives. **"God is faithful; he will not let you be tempted beyond what you can bear. But when you are tempted, he will also provide a way out so that you can stand up under it."** (1 Corinthians 10:13)

In the course of your lifetime, you will meet many people who believe that the Bible is an outdated, archaic book that doesn't really apply to us anymore in this day and age. They'll say, for example: *"Come on, I have nothing in common with Abraham, Moses, David, or Paul. They didn't have my high pressured job. They didn't struggle with paying their mortgage, or have to drive my traffic-congested commute. They didn't have to deal with my stubborn boss or my rebellious kids. Besides, our society is much more complex now. The rules need to change to adapt to the times. How could the Bible apply to my life today, just as much as it did to people thousands of years ago? There's no way."* But, if we remember that there is truly nothing new under the sun, that everything we experience and wrestle with is actually, in its most basic form, the very same stuff that all people have dealt with since the beginning of time, it helps us understand that we really can relate to Biblical characters after all. We have the same emotions, struggles, concerns, and temptations. And that means that the Word of God is every bit as relevant to you and I today as it was 3,000+ years ago. God didn't just write the Bible for a certain culture or group of people, long, long ago. It was written for you and me, right here, *today*!

That is a vital connection that we'll want to help others understand and fully embrace. Once they see the relevance of God's Word to their lives, they will be more willing to listen to it.

I have always imagined the Biblical character Samson to be like *The Incredible Hulk*. (Samson has an interesting story, which I encourage you to read in Judges chapters 13-16.) Now, while only one of them is green, and the other has freakishly long hair because he never had it cut, both men have surreal physical strength combined with the inability to control their temper. I can picture in my mind's eye Samson uttering the Hulk's most famous line: "You're making me angry... You won't like me when I'm angry!" Both Samson and The Hulk could use a little *Anger Management* from Jack Nicholson. Not being able to control one's anger has destroyed leaders throughout human history.

However, in the 2008 movie, *The Incredible Hulk*, we notice an interesting development in the Hulk's mild-mannered alter ego. Bruce Banner has started to figure himself out. He realizes that if he wants to avoid situations that will make him angry (thereby triggering the trans-formation into the Hulk), he needs to use forethought and good judgment. For example, he knows that it would not be a wise thing to go into a crowded subway. When his girlfriend suggests it, he replies: "Me, in a metal tube, deep under-ground, with hundreds of people in the most aggressive city in the world?!" She agrees that it wouldn't be a wise decision, and they take a cab instead. We see that Bruce is beginning to understand himself. He is learning how to control his heart rate and to avoid certain situations that will lead to trouble. Bruce is learning how to cope with his weaknesses.

How different the Samson story would have played out if only he had learned a little more about himself and his shortcomings! Samson had the potential to be a great leader and warrior. His girlfriend Delilah certainly wouldn't have been a problem if he knew himself a little bit better. He might have lived a much happier (and certainly longer) life, but instead he died a blinded prisoner (Judges 16). And before you think that "blindness" isn't your problem, know that Satan wants you to think exactly that. He loves to blind us to our own sin. This is one of his most effective and insidious tactics. God has equipped us with the gifts, skills, and abilities to avoid and fight every kind of temptation, but often it is our "spiritual blindness" that gets us into trouble.

Moses was a reluctant leader of God's people. God spoke to him through a dramatic display of a burning bush, but Moses kept making excuses as to why he couldn't do what God wanted him to do. Aragorn is a reluctant leader in *The Lord of the Rings* trilogy. He doesn't want to be king, but it is precisely who he is called to be. Arthur, in the movie *King Arthur,* is another reluctant leader. But he, too, is the one chosen for the job. Here's an interesting point to note: King Arthur was able to accomplish what he did in the movie because he was both a Roman and a Brit. In the *Indiana Jones* saga, we see that what makes Indy unique is that he is both a devoted teacher and an archeologist/adventurer. Moses was chosen in part because he was both a Hebrew and an Egyptian. St. Paul was selected for his significant role partly because he was a Roman citizen of Jewish decent. God loves dual citizenship – so much, in fact, that He gave it to His own Son! Jesus is true God and true man. And remember, God created YOU as both a citizen of planet earth *and*, through Baptism, a citizen of heaven. Even when we are reluctant to follow the paths that God has set before us, it is encouraging to know He will work in us and through us to accomplish His purposes. We will be **"thoroughly equipped for every good work."** (2 Timothy 3:17)

Does one of your favorite movie characters remind you of a particular character from the Bible? That could open the door for an interesting spiritual discussion. Your friend might not even know who Abraham, Job, Ruth, David, Judas, Peter, and Paul are! Just think – many of the Sunday School stories that you've known since childhood might be completely new and intriguing stories to your friends who don't yet know Jesus.

And remember, you don't have to worry that you might not have all the answers. You certainly don't have to know every Biblical story perfectly. Think of it as a great excuse to open the Bible together to research the story. The most important thing you need to know is this: Jesus is our salvation and our hope. We might have to research and look up the small details, and that is perfectly fine. We don't have to be Biblical scholars – we just love Jesus and want to know Him better and share Him with the world. In this way, we will **"always be prepared to give an answer to everyone who asks you to give the reason for the hope that you have."** (1 Peter 3:15)

A word of warning as you look for relatable Biblical characters in the films that you watch – it's often too easy to compare a movie character to Jesus. Remember that Jesus was the only perfect person that ever walked upon the earth. Any semblance to Jesus will fall indescribably short because Jesus is beyond any human parallel. In literature there is a concept of the "Christ figure" – the character that makes a sacrifice. While that's fine in literature, this concept is not quite as simple in your vocation as an Evangelist/Translator.

Scripture tells us that **"Jesus Christ is the same yesterday and today and forever."** (Hebrews 13:8) All I have to do is show you my high school year book to prove that no human being can claim that! Jesus is one of a kind. Several movies over the years have tried to show God in human form, such as the *Oh God* movies of the 70s and 80s starring an ancient-looking George Burns as God, or Kevin Smith's Alanis Morissette as God in *Dogma,* or Morgan Freeman who plays God in *Bruce Almighty* and *Evan*

Almighty. None of them shows even a glimmer of the power, might, and authority of our God – the one true God! People may do Christ-like things, but no human being is worthy of a comparison to Jesus. This important truth can be used as a great evangelism tool in itself.

Think about all the names given to Jesus: Wonderful Counselor, Mighty God, Everlasting Father, Prince of Peace, Redeemer, Savior, Lord, King... I could go on and on. Perhaps a movie character exhibits those qualities. While no one is like Jesus, we can use certain characteristics to *point* to Jesus.

For example, my young daughters love watching movies. Occasionally, they are even willing to watch a movie that isn't from the "princess" genre. They have a ton of questions throughout each movie, but they love to watch them. Our church had planned a night to go see the second Narnia movie, *Prince Caspian.* My daughters, 3 and 5 years old at the time, really wanted to go. While it was rated PG, I debated whether to take them. I wasn't sure if they would like it and, more importantly, we need to do everything we can at this point in life to avoid bad dreams. So, I thought we'd rent *The Chronicles of Narnia: The Lion, The Witch and the Wardrobe* first.

It turns out that they loved *Narnia.* It also turns out that they had a lot of questions and comments (surprise, surprise). Two particular observations just blew me away:

First, when the White Witch came on the scene, I gave them the heads-up that she was the "Mean Witch." I have learned from past experience (with Cinderella, Snow White, Sleeping Beauty, and pretty much every princess movie ever made) that my daughters greatly appreciate knowing in advance who the Mean Witch is in the story. But the Mean Witch in Narnia is different. Maile, my five-year-old, responded to my heads-up with: "Daddy, she can't be the Mean Witch – she's so beautiful!"

Wow, she really thought that something evil had to be ugly. What an understanding of this world. Attractive things are good. Ugly things are bad. Satan used this trick in the Garden of Eden (Genesis 3:1-6), and he's still using the same trick all the time. Scripture calls him **"an angel of light."** (2 Corinthians 11:14) Satan and his ways can look very attractive. They can even look healthy and good at times, but they are meant to destroy. Beauty can be very deceiving. Satan was played by a supermodel in the movie remake *Bedazzled*, and by Al Pacino in *The Devil's Advocate*. (I guess some people think he's attractive.) And as Meryl Streep reminds us, *The Devil Wears Prada*. To be honest, I'm not really sure what Prada is, but it sounds really expensive!

The second Narnia observation from my five-year-old came when the great Lion, Aslan, gives himself over to the White Witch and her minions to fulfill the ancient law and to redeem Edmund. It's a pretty scary and tense time in the movie. So, again, being a good, loving father, it was heads-up time. "Maile," I said, "They are going to kill Aslan, but don't worry because he's going to come back to life – just like Jesus."

"Yeah, Daddy," she said, "but Jesus is so much better!"

What wisdom at five years old! Jesus is best. The world will try to trick us with its "Turkish Delight," and the world will succeed much of the time. But as we share our movie observations with others, always remember this important truth: no one can compare to Jesus.

I Saw You in the Movie

Most of us, at some point in our lives, dream of being a big-time movie star. My two little girls have been acting, dancing, singing, and performing in their very own shows from the moment they could talk. Maile asks me all the time when she's going to be big enough to be on TV. While very, very few of our silver screen dreams ever come true, we can spark some interesting and lively conversations when we tell our friends that we saw a character that reminded us of them. Let the fun begin as they agree or disagree with your character analysis!

The reason that a simple, low-budget movie like *The Breakfast Club* has so much staying power is that it's relatively easy for us to see our friends in it. There are no explosions, car chases or special effects in this movie – it just deals with high school life. High school is an inevitable (although not always enjoyable) part of growing up. Regardless of how long it's been since I've graduated, nothing can take me back to the sights, sounds, smells, and memories of high school like a movie about teenage angst.

The Breakfast Club reminds us of those we knew in school – the jock, the nerd, the rebel, the princess, and the outcast – and where we fit into the social strata. Those well-defined identities seemed so important back then. Is it possible for nerds and jocks to get along? Can the rebel actually date the prom queen?

The characters in *The Breakfast Club* focus on their individual differences in the beginning of the movie, but by the end an interesting thing happens. They realize that although they come from different cliques, different parts of town, and different walks of life, they're really much more similar than they ever imagined. At the conclusion of the movie, they leave their detention essay assignment on the desk, which has evolved throughout the movie to read: "Dear Mr. Vernon, we accept the fact that we had to sacrifice a whole Saturday in detention for whatever it was we did wrong. But we think you're crazy to make us write an essay telling you who we think we are. You see us as you want to see us – in the simplest terms and the most convenient definitions. But what we found out is that each one of us is a brain ... and an athlete ... and a basket case ... a princess ... and a criminal ... Does that answer your question? Sincerely yours, the Breakfast Club."

They're different, yet somehow the same. Kind of like every human culture on the face of the planet! We tend to focus on the differences between us, but we all share our humanity. And like the theme song says, the members of the Breakfast Club don't want to be forgotten. We all want our lives to be significant. We all want to love, and to be loved. Movies like *The Breakfast Club* that remind us of our common ground can provide a great opportunity for us to tell our friends that God loves us, regardless of our backgrounds. He has put each of us in this world for a meaningful purpose.

On a slightly different note, do you see your friends in *High School Musical*? Many people thought the movie musical genre was dead because no one naturally breaks into spontaneous song these days. But those people were dead wrong! *HSM* has been a huge success. Why? Different cliques coming together is a main theme in the *HSM* movies. In one of the director's commentaries on the *HSM* DVDs, we learn that it was his goal to establish each of the characters in the movie as a high school stereotype so that every viewer could find someone they could relate to. He knew that he could capture more imaginations if people saw themselves and their friends in the film. However, an interesting twist is that a major theme in all of these movies is the realization that each one of us is more complex than a stereotype or label. At the end of *High School Musical 3: Senior Year,* Troy is being pressured to choose between musical theater and sports... again... but this time, it's for college. Man, the stakes get higher each time! And once again, Troy chooses... both. He isn't going to let a stereotype like "jock" or "drama geek" hold him back. He wants to break free from the expectations of others and follow the path of his own choosing.

Do you know anyone who can relate to struggling with feelings of being labeled? Do you know anyone who thinks God could never care about them because they are a social outcast? Tell them that God shatters such labels when we put our trust in the only perfect person who's ever lived – Jesus Christ. God doesn't want us to go through life burdened under the weight of our inadequacies. **"Come to me, all you who are weary and burdened, and I will give you rest."** (Matthew 11:28)

Let's move away from the teen movies and into one of my favorite subcategories: the "buddy cop" movie. When you watch *Lethal Weapon, 48 Hours, Running Scared, Tango and Cash, Bad Boys,* or even the buddy cop movie spoof – *Cop Out* – do you see *your* buddy? Is your buddy the good cop or the bad cop? Is he the suave ladies man or the loving family man? Is he steady and loyal, or wild and crazy? When asked about his mismatched partner, Roger Murtaugh in *Lethal Weapon* says, "God hates me. That's what it is." Sorry Roger, but you're together for a distinct purpose. God has a reason for putting *our* buddies into our life, too! You may not always recognize it right away, but He's got a purpose.

While these buddy cop movies all have different pairings, the ending is always the same: opposites come together and after a series of mishaps, realize that their differences are actually their strengths. We're all different – praise God for that! – but it is important that we understand that Jesus loves us despite our differences. St. Paul makes a bold statement in Galatians 3:28 – **"There is neither Jew nor Greek, slave nor free, male nor female, for you are all one in Christ Jesus."** Jesus created us to be unique, and yet He reminds us that we are all one. No matter who we are, Jesus loves us.

The Inside Scoop

My friends have been telling me for years that I remind them of Brad Pitt. While I'll be the first to admit that there are many obvious physical similarities, I do hope you're smarter than my friends. Seeing your friends and family in a movie isn't about outward looks, but personality, attitude, charisma – the stuff on the inside. Your mom always told you not to judge a book by its cover, and she was right. What's most important is our character. But we also know that inside each of us is a sinful nature that can only be cleaned by the blood of Jesus. This is one of the reasons I love to witness baptisms. In baptism we get to experience the cleaning on the *inside*. Just as my daughter Maile was delighted to get drenched in the aptly named "Soak Zone" at Sea World, we too are blessed at our baptism in a way we'll never forget (even if baptized as an infant). Holy Baptism is not about the water. It's not about the amount, temperature, location, or "holiness" of the water. The water isn't special at all. It's about an encounter – a connection with Jesus for all eternity. It's a cleansing on the inside, through the powerful, life-changing Word of God. In the classic 80s movie *Overboard*, when Goldie Hawn falls off the boat into the water, she becomes a completely new person. She has completely forgotten her old self. In baptism, we completely forget our old self. It's the experience of forgiveness. It's the promise of life everlasting. And it's the reminder that God desires the whole world to come to Him through the continually flowing waters of baptism.

There is a saying that sums up so much of our life in Christ – "Jesus loves you just the way you are, but he loves you too much to keep you that way." Jesus has a dream for your life that is beyond whatever you yourself can imagine. Just as a poorly developed character usually leads to a bad movie, a lack of strong character development in our own lives may lead to negative consequences and a troubled, unfulfilling life. We need guidance along life's journey, and Jesus is just The Director to develop our character to its maximum potential.

In fact, we read in Mark 6:39 that **"Jesus directed them."** Now, while that quote may be taken a little out of context, the metaphor of Jesus as our Director is still a powerful one. Jesus wants to be the Director of your life! However, He's not going to force His will upon you. You have been given free will. And remember, free will is a gift, not a curse. God *wants* you to make your own choices. He doesn't want you to be a robot. God gave you a brain for a reason, and He wants you to use it. We all have the ability to select the paths we take, and to choose between right and wrong. He has given us His Word to guide us in those decisions (Psalm 119:105), and He promises to be with us always (Matthew 28:20). St. Paul reminds us in Philippians 4:13: **"I can do everything through him who gives me strength."** It's not about us. It's about Jesus, the Director, working in us and through us. When we allow Jesus to be our Director, the movie of our life will be much more fulfilling, God-pleasing, and meaningful. Like the title character said in *Jerry Maguire*: "This is going to change everything!" By listening to the Director, there will be powerful changes in our lives – and get ready for the lives of those around us to change, too!

Pray about It

- Pray that God will strengthen your character.

Talk about It

- What are some of your favorite movie characters? Which type of character do you usually relate to? The hero? The villain? The sidekick? The lovable loser? The outcast?

- King Solomon wrote that **"there is nothing new under the sun."** (Ecclesiastes 1:9) Do you think we have more or less temptations nowadays than in Biblical times? How has Satan's "bag of tricks" evolved with the times?

- Can you think of a movie character who reminds you of Moses? Paul? Ruth? Esther? David? Other Biblical characters?

Live It Out

- Randomly grab a DVD from your collection and go through the main characters. Try to find a Biblical character that can relate to each one of them.

- Paul tells us in Philippians 4:13, **"I can do everything through him who gives me strength."** What are some ways that you've clearly seen God's strength working through you? Are there things that you hesitate to try because you don't feel spiritually strong enough to do them? For many, evangelism ranks high on that list. Write down the areas in your life in which you feel you are weak. Pray for God's strength and encouragement in those areas. Resolve to try one new thing this week that takes you out of your "comfort zone."

Talking Pictures Example #6

Hanging out in the living room, flipping through the channels, we stumbled upon something all too familiar. "*The Breakfast Club* is on *again*?" I groaned, laughing.

"I know it! If I had a nickel for every time it's on TV, I'd be rich!" my teenage cousin, Julie, exclaimed.

"Someone has made a lot more than a nickel for every time it's on," I added. "I think this movie made loads of people rich – and launched a lot of acting careers."

"I have to admit that every time it's on, I can't change the channel!" Julie confessed. "I just gotta watch it!"

"Why's that?" I asked as I settled back onto the couch, realizing this was going to be our afternoon activity. "I know – you just love those 80s fashions!"

"Well of course!" she laughed. "But I think this is just one of those movies that makes you happy to be yourself – whoever you are – like the nerd, the jock, the princess, whatever. This movie helps you understand that it's okay to be you. Everyone hurts. Everyone has issues. Nobody's perfect, and that's okay. You know, *that* kind of stuff."

"That's kind of deep for four o'clock in the afternoon!" I teased her.

"No, seriously," Julie continued thoughtfully. "I'm not one of those chicks who cries at movies. But this one usually gets me started, even though I've probably seen it a million times."

"I know what you mean," I replied more seriously. "This world is a tough place to find your place in life. That's why this movie has so much appeal. It's fun to watch six people each find their place in the span of two hours."

"That would be so cool if it happened that way in real life," she sighed.

My mind was buzzing, sensing that an opportunity to share the Gospel might be at hand. "Maybe we don't find our place because we're looking in the wrong spot," I suggested. "I mean, detention isn't exactly where you'd expect to find your place in life. But they do! That's kinda the whole point of the movie, isn't it?"

She turned toward me curiously. "Why do you say that?"

"Because, in the movie, the location doesn't matter as much as what happens there. Their personal walls come down and they're honest with each other." I paused for a moment. "What if we could all be open and honest with each other? What if we could just be ourselves?"

"Honesty's a difficult thing," she admitted. "We gotta look cool and say the right thing. If you open up too much, you might get hurt. It's hard. We gotta blend into the crowd and still try to find a way to be who we really are."

"Sure, but what if we could just be free from all that?" I wondered aloud.

"It would be great to have that freedom!" Julie sat up excitedly. I knew it had been a tough year for her in a new high school – trying to fit into the crowd.

I continued, hoping she would be receptive to hearing more. "But isn't *The Breakfast Club* really about freedom? Free to be who you really are, not who someone else wants you to be? I think we can all find that freedom. But it doesn't come from a place – it comes from a person. It comes from

Jesus! You can have the freedom to be who you are, to accept yourself for who God created you to be. Jesus loves you no matter what social group you're in... or think you need to belong to."

"Okay, okay, now you're getting too into religion!" Julie laughed nervously.

I softened my approach a bit. "Well, I know it's been a difficult year for you. And I want you to know that you can feel good about yourself and be your own person. Other people don't define who you are, Julie. It's not what crowd you hang out with or what label people put on you. You're an amazing person just the way you are, because Jesus loves you and died for you."

"Ummm... okay, but can we just watch the movie?" She smiled sheepishly at me and shifted in her seat.

I could tell that she was uncomfortable, and I knew it would be better to let my words settle for awhile. I quickly switched gears. "Yes, of course!" I laughed, reaching for the remote. Then I gently added, "I just want you to know I care about you, and that I'm praying for you and want to help however I can."

"Thanks." She smiled and relaxed a little. "I don't pray, but I'm sure it can't hurt, right? Thanks for caring about what I'm going through. Maybe we can talk more about all this stuff after the movie is over."

Take 2

Relatable Situations

Movies are full of relatable situations. Okay, so maybe the fate of the entire world has never rested in your hands, like John McClane in *Die Hard* or Will Smith in *Independence Day*. But you've probably experienced plenty of challenges, pressures, and difficult decisions in your own life. As we watch the action unfold in a film, it's fun to ponder how we ourselves would handle a similar situation. Perhaps we would make the same decisions as the character. Maybe we would do the complete opposite. Would we jump on that grenade to save our friends? Would we have the courage and conviction to stand up to the bully who's picking on the school outcast? Would we have the confidence to ask out the really attractive girl at work that everyone says is out of our league? When the moment of truth arrives, what will we decide to do?

Been There and Done That

What would you do if you were outnumbered a thousand to one, like the Spartans in *300*? Would you run away? Would you join the side with the bigger army? As King Leonidas said, "Remember this day, men, for it will be yours for all time." This kind of dramatic situation makes us think about what is truly significant in our own lives. What will you remember, and what will you be remembered for? In our natural human desire for significance, we all want to leave a legacy behind. What will your legacy be?

How would you handle the situation of the wrongful death of your parents? Would that drive you to become Batman (or at the very least, Robin)? Director Christopher Nolan took over the Batman franchise in 2005 with *Batman Begins*. His follow-up film, *The Dark Knight* (the first Batman movie not to have the word "Batman" in the title) became the highest grossing movie of 2008. Comic book movies are a very popular genre, but how did this one get to be so huge? I believe *The Dark Knight* did so well at the box office because it is filled with many "What would I do?" moments. There are quite a few moral dilemmas in the movie. Is it okay to commit a crime if it is done for the greater good? Is violence permissible if it ultimately leads to peace? Should I kill other innocent people to save myself? Lines are crossed throughout the movie. Even wise old Alfred, Batman's trusted butler and best friend, has to tell him that even though he's the hero, he crossed the line first. Perhaps the question that overshadows all others is this: Is Batman truly a hero? In the very last line of the movie, Commissioner Gordon tells his son: "Because he's the hero Gotham deserves, but not the one it needs right now. So we'll hunt him because he can take it. Because he's not our hero. He's a silent guardian, a watchful protector. A dark knight." There are so many difficult situations throughout the movie, and the audience is compelled to reflect on each dilemma.

Life is full of choices. Even seemingly insignificant choices can have big consequences. What would I do? What *should* I do? A powerful movie will engage the viewer's imagination and prod him or her to ask these questions repeatedly throughout the course of the film. A movie's strength might very well lie in the number of opportunities we have to ask ourselves such questions.

What would you do if wild, supernatural things started happening – as they did to Ben Stiller in *Night at the Museum* – but when you told others about them, no one would believe you? The dinosaur comes to life and wants to play fetch. Attila the Hun is amused by your tricks but then wants to rip all of your limbs off when he learns they're only illusions. Tiny cowboys and Roman soldiers continue to wage war on each other even though you helped them agree to a peace treaty. Just another typical night at work for Ben Stiller! The events in this movie may seem far-fetched, but think about this: Jesus is constantly working miracles in our lives. If your friends don't believe it, maybe, like Ben Stiller, you need to bring them in for a closer look. Show them exactly what's going on. Share with them the blessings and changes that Christ is working in your life and in your world. Changed lives change lives. How can you show your friends the miracles that are happening in your life?

What would you do if you came into possession of the "one ring to rule them all?" Would you become Gollum or Frodo? Would you turn into the selfish villain? Would you be wise enough to know your limits and just avoid the ring altogether? Would you be willing to give up its powers? As many have discovered throughout history, power can be a very difficult thing to surrender. In *The Fellowship of the Ring*, the first movie in *The Lord of the Rings* trilogy, Gandalf realizes this and states: "I dare not take it. Not even to keep it safe. Understand, Frodo. I would use this ring from a desire to do good. But through me, it would wield a power too great and terrible to imagine." Would you have the wisdom and strength to set aside your own gain for the greater good? Temptation is a major part of life. And the closer we get to Jesus, the harder Satan is going to work to make us fall. We have to be on our guard, and like Gandalf, we need to know and recognize our weaknesses. Do you honestly know your weaknesses?

What would you do if you suddenly became rich beyond your wildest dreams? How would this completely change your life? If money was no longer a concern for you, which parts of your life would you keep, and which would you leave behind? What are the things that are so important to you that no amount of money could ever change them? What would you do if you suddenly stumbled upon millions of dollars that didn't belong to you? Would you be tempted to keep it or would you return it? Could you live a lie? What happened in *Millions*? What happened in *Blank Check*? What happened in *A Simple Plan*? Those are just a few of the movies that feature this situation. It's a classic moral dilemma in the lives of both Christians and non-Christians alike: should you keep something that doesn't belong to you? Interestingly enough, the characters in each of these movies all handle the situation a bit differently.

Before you stand up and shout at the top of your lungs, "Show me the money!" like Rod Tidwell in *Jerry Maguire*, remember that Jesus never said that money is the root of all evil. Although He is often quoted as saying that, it's not what Scripture says. St. Paul tells us that **"the *love* of money is a root of all kinds of evil."** (1 Timothy 6:10) Simply put – you can't love both God and money. Lots of people have tried, but no one has ever succeeded. It goes back to the first commandment, which states that we must have no other gods besides our one true God. Money can very quickly become a god. No matter what Gordon Gekko says in *Wall Street*, greed is never good. In fact, greed has ruined famous leaders and crumbled massive empires since the world began. How would you handle the temptation of greed?

Thanks be to God that Jesus can relate to every situation we will ever face! Jesus was tempted in every way that we are, yet never sinned: **"For we do not have a high priest who is unable to sympathize with our weaknesses, but we have one who has been tempted in every way, just as we are – yet was without sin."** (Hebrews 4:15) Not only is this a huge comfort to us in the trials and tribulations we will face in our lives, but it also gives us a powerful tool for evangelism. Whatever situation we see and relate to on the silver screen, we have a Savior who can relate. Jesus has been there, done that, and has the scars to prove it! While it's great to ask "What would I do?" we need to focus on – and rejoice in – what Jesus has *already* done. Even though we face the struggles of life in this world, we have the confidence that the battle has already been won for us in Christ.

Our faith is not about who we are, or what we do. It's about Jesus, and what He has done for us on the cross. Nike has had a very successful, long-running marketing campaign with the slogan, "Just Do It™." In fact, it's been so popular that many people have tried to use "Just Do It" as a slogan for their lives! But I like the life-slogan that St. Paul gives us in 1 Thessalonians 5:24b much better: ***"he* will do it."** Jesus will do it. He did it for you in the manger. He did it for you in the desert when Satan came tempting. He did it for you on the cross. He did it for you in the empty tomb. And He's doing it for you right now as He reigns in heaven. Whatever difficult or challenging situations you may face in your life, He will be there for you!

Disasters of Biblical Proportions

As you are Talking Pictures with your friends, re-member that those who don't know Jesus yet may not realize the relatable situations that so many of the Bible's characters were living in. To keep the spiritual conversations going, let's try using a Biblical character to relate to that pivotal moment or conflict-filled situation in the movie. Connecting these two points will help your friend understand the relevance of Scripture in our lives.

Who was more shocked: Luke Skywalker, when he found out in *Star Wars: Episode V – The Empire Strikes Back* that his enemy, Darth Vader, was actually his father, or St.

Paul (then Saul), when a brilliant light came down from heaven and God informed him that he was persecuting His people (Acts 9:1-31)? Each had a huge awakening to a whole new sense of reality. Luke lost his hand and Paul was temporarily blinded. Yet both were "healed" and did quite a bit of "converting." In *Star Wars: Episode VI – The Return of the Jedi*, Luke told his father that he would save him. To this, Darth Vader's last words were: "You already have, Luke." Likewise, Paul says in 2 Timothy 4:7, **"I have fought the good fight, I have finished the race, I have kept the faith."** They both received their "salvation!"

How does Spiderman wrestling with the evil Venom in *Spiderman 3* compare with Jacob wrestling with God (Genesis 32:24-31)? Both Spiderman and Jacob learned that they were also wrestling with themselves and their own sinful desires. In describing his "wrestling match," Peter Parker says in Spiderman 3: "Whatever comes our way, whatever battle we have raging inside us, we always have a choice. My friend Harry taught me that. He chose to be the best of himself. It's the choices that make us who we are, and we can always choose to do what's right." Throughout time, human choices have led to quite a bit of unnecessary conflict and suffering. Chaotic and difficult events are common in Scripture, in the movies, and in the world around us. Yet, ultimately we know that God is at work even during the challenging times.

What are some ways we can take a powerful situation in a movie, and relate it back to the Holy Bible? The Bible is the main avenue through which we know the heart of God. It's the true and inspired Word of God, written through human hands. By God's grace, we should aim to bring our conversations back to the message of the Bible, and the reason for the hope we have in Christ (1 Peter 3:15). This is the translator part of the Evangelist/Translator job description.

In the movie *The Day After Tomorrow*, the world has gone into another ice age. In the traumatic events that follow,

Jake Gyllenhaal and his father are separated, but his dad promises to come get him – no matter what. As catastrophes continue to strike and things become increasingly difficult, the hope of rescue starts to fade. Jake's friends begin to doubt that his father is coming back, but Jake just smiles and tells them, "You don't know my father!" People who don't have a relationship with God don't understand our Heavenly Father. They don't understand how much He loves them, and that He wants to rescue them from the desperate consequences of their unbelief. The best way to help your friends know God is to lead them to the Source – i.e., get them directly plugged into His Word.

By the way, in *The Day After Tomorrow*, Jake's dad does show up after all of his friends have given up hope – just when they least expect it, and just when they need it most. Your Heavenly Father will do the same for you. He is omnipresent, so He's there even when you don't see Him or feel Him. But often He will reveal Himself when you least expect it and most need it. In *The Lord of the Rings*, we learn that a wizard is never early and never late. Likewise, God's timing is always perfect. His presence is perfect. So keep your eyes and ears open. God desires all people to know Him (1 Timothy 2:4).

One of the unique things about the Bible, compared to the "holy books" of other religions, is that it shows the warts and weaknesses of its characters – much as a good movie does. Scripture shows us the failures and shortcomings of God's people in addition to their successes. Nobody's perfect – not even the Biblical giants of faith! For example, Moses is revered for being the leader of the Exodus, but he was a murderer as well (Exodus 2:12). The Bible tells us that Moses struggled with a speech impediment (Exodus 4:10) and often lacked confidence (e.g., Exodus 3:11 and 4:1). And near the end of his life, he became *too* confident, and so was not allowed to enter the Promised Land (Numbers 20:7-12).

Scripture allows us to see these Biblical heroes as ordinary, flawed human beings, just like you and me, by providing their "backstory." Showing the backstory is a technique used in movies to show the history and humanity of the characters.

Indiana Jones's fear of snakes was explained in a backstory that opened *Indiana Jones and the Last Crusade*. In that movie you also met Indy's father, which provided even more depth into the character. Some of the best backstories we see in films are those belonging to the villain characters. Maybe the villain isn't really so bad; he's just mourning the loss of his brother, like in *Die Hard: With a Vengeance*. We learn in the film version of *Dr. Suess's How The Grinch Stole Christmas* that the Grinch was mistreated and picked on as a youngster, which led to his "grinchiness" in adulthood. In *The Dark Knight* we learn how the Joker got his facial scars. His father had sadistically cut him... or did he? Is it possible that the Joker lied to try to get us to feel sorry for him? Villains are often the most interesting characters in movies, especially when we are able to see their backstory. There's something that helps us relate better when we realize that we are all shaped by our circumstances.

Hollywood uses the backstory technique to give us a full picture of the character and an insight into why they make the choices they do. In much the same way, the entire Old Testament serves as the backstory of Jesus. It answers the question of why we need a Savior, and presents us with God's solution – His own Son, born of his infinite love. The New Testament then fulfills that promise of a Savior in Jesus.

Too Close for Comfort

Watching movies can be a cathartic experience. When people can relate to the situations they see on screen and it touches them in a deeply personal way, feelings and painful emotions have a chance to be expressed.

There are few things more heartbreaking in youth ministry than watching a student endure the pain and grief of losing a parent. There are no "right" words to say after a tragic event like that. The overwhelming question that weighs on our hearts and minds is: "*Why?*" But all of the standard answers to that question do not do enough to ease the pain: "They're in a better place." "You'll see them again someday." "You'll understand why someday." "Bad things can happen to good people." "Death is a natural part of life." All are appropriate answers, and Biblical as well. But sometimes when someone is grieving, words are inadequate. The most helpful support might be just to mourn with them. Jesus cried with his friends when Lazarus died – even though He knew He was going to raise Lazarus from the dead! Jesus wept because He saw his friends in pain, and He shared in their grief (John 11:35). Often, the best thing you can do for a grieving friend is to love them in their time of pain and mourning. Be there for them, especially after the rest of the crowd has dispersed and gone back to the routines of life.

A few months after one boy in my youth ministry, a fifth grader, lost his mother to cancer, his friends took him to see the movie *Stepmom*. At the time, it really surprised me that his friends would take him to this particular movie. The movie is basically the story of two children who watch their mother die of cancer shortly after their father remarries. It would be adequately filed under the movie genre of "tear-jerker." It was a very emotional experience for my student, and he cried through much of the movie. His friends felt extremely guilty for taking him to see it. However, I think his friends were trying to do something beautiful to help him through his grief. They knew it was something he could relate to, and in a way that only someone else who has gone through that experience could. Watching movies can help our friends to open up about things we might not normally be willing to discuss with others. These situations give us a greater opportunity to share the Gospel with others. Our friends will be more receptive to the help and hope that Jesus offers during the difficult times.

Human beings for the most part like to be in charge. However, as we all know too well, life cannot always be controlled. We like to think we're in control of everything that happens to us, but we're not. Adam Sandler made a whole movie about this concept. In *Click*, he visits the "Way Beyond" section of his local Bed, Bath & Beyond Superstore, and finds a remote control that controls his entire life. He is able to fast-forward through the boring parts of life, and pause to savor the good stuff. But he soon learns that much of the joy is taken out of his life when he is always in control. Joy comes to us in the small, seemingly insignificant moments – not just in the big stuff. The world may tell us not to sweat the small stuff, but who determines what's small and what's not? St. Paul reminds us, in one of the shortest verses in the Bible – **"Be joyful always."** (1 Thessalonians 5:16) Even when life has no rhyme or reason, and everything seems beyond our grasp, we can still be joyful in all circumstances because we know that God *is* in control!

Think about that for a minute. *Nothing* is out of God's control! Peace and understanding come when we put our trust in Him. We have to trust that tragedy is God's opportunity. Yes, bad things do happen to "good" people. Most of us have trouble understanding this, because we view it as unfair. But when bad things do happen, it has very little to do with the degree of "goodness" of the person, and everything to do with the sinful and fallen state of the world in which we live. And yet, when a spouse is killed in a car accident, a child is born with severe disabilities, or a hurricane leaves death and devastation in its path, we ask, "Why?" People will give you all kinds of answers, but let's be honest, no one really knows why. I think that pretending to have an answer does more harm than good. There is power is simply stating, "I don't know, but Jesus is still in control." There is comfort in an honest reply of: "I don't have all the answers, but I have the truth, **'and the truth will set you free'** (John 8:32)!" Jesus is the way, the truth and the life (John 14:6). In Him there is freedom. And as the wise, blue Genie from *Aladdin* reminds us: "To be free... such a thing would be greater than all the magic and treasures in all the world." We constantly find ourselves chasing magic and treasure in our lives. But the greatest gift – which is already ours – is the freedom found in Christ!

All things and all situations happen for a reason. As St. Paul's letter to the Christians in Rome reminds us – **"we know that in all things God works for the good of those who love him."** (Romans 8:28) *All* things work out for good. Not just the positive, upbeat stuff – but everything! The "love" and the "trust" can be the difficult parts. Love and trust take a considerable amount of time and energy. Love and trust can end in large amounts of pain and frustration. But that's why we're Talking Pictures in the first place. By God's grace we want to help our friends get to the point where they can love and trust Jesus. There is an eternal significance!

At the end of the movie *Charlie Wilson's War*, a story is told of a boy in a small village with a Zen master. The boy received a horse as a fourteenth birthday present, and all the people in the village were so happy for him and talked about how lucky this boy was. But the Zen master simply said, "We'll see." Shortly after that, the boy fell off of his horse and broke his leg. Everyone in the village was so sad over this unfortunate accident and declared that this boy was incredibly unlucky. But the Master just said, "We'll see." Shortly thereafter, the country was drawn into a horrible, brutal war and all able-bodied boys were forced to go off to war. However, the boy couldn't go because of his leg. The village folk declared how lucky this boy was for not having to go to war. And – you guessed it – the Zen master said... "We'll see."

God sees! Even when we don't see or understand, God sees the big picture. Our perception of things is not the same as God's. In His miraculous, unexplainable way, He somehow works ultimate good out of every single situation – even when bad things happen to good people, and even when we screw up and squander the wonderful blessings He has given us. God handles the small stuff, the big stuff, and everything in-between, and He never even breaks a sweat! We don't understand how it works. We can't begin to explain how He takes care of all people at all times and in all places. We can't always see it in the midst of difficulties. But faith is believing in what we can't see (Hebrews 11:1). It doesn't matter if we don't have all the answers, as long as we love God and trust in Him. For some things, we may have to wait until heaven for it all to work out. But there is great joy and comfort in knowing that it *will* work out! There is an eternally happy ending for all those who are connected to Jesus. Let's do everything we can, through the Holy Spirit's power, to enable our friends to come to know Him as well, that they may receive the same peace, comfort, and gift of salvation that we know in Christ!

Pray about It

- Pray that God will give you wisdom to know what to do and say in any situation.

Talk about It

- Think about your favorite movies. Which ones contain situations that you can relate to personally?

- What are some ways we can take a dramatic situation in a movie and relate it back to the Bible?

- How are movies cathartic? How can a movie help someone open up and express their feelings?

- Even though we know that God is in control, we often tend to worry and fret over all of the little details of our lives. However, Romans 8:28 reminds us **"that in all things God works for the good of those who love him, who have been called according to his purpose."** Why is it so hard for us to let go and entrust our problems, concerns, and fears to our Heavenly Father?

Live It Out

- Make plans to invite another non-Christian friend from the list you made at the beginning of this book to come see a movie with you this week. Look through movie descriptions and reviews online, and try to find one that contains a storyline or situation that your friend will readily identify with. Pray for windows of opportunity to open during your post-movie conversations. Pray for God's wisdom and guidance, and for your friend to be receptive to the message you convey.

Talking Pictures Example #7

"Are you sure you want to see *Star Trek?*" Jim asked me, squinting up at the theater marquee as we waited in line for our tickets. "I know it got good reviews, but come on – after 50 years, how can they still boldly go where no man has gone before?"

I laughed at my friend's sense of humor. "Don't worry," I assured him. "You're going to love this movie! I saw it at midnight on opening night. Remember, this isn't your father's *Star Trek!*"

"If I don't like this movie," he paused dramatically and looked me straight in the eye, "I'm holding *you* personally responsible!"

"I'll take that responsibility," I laughed. "This movie has it all – action, comedy, romance, adventure. You won't be disappointed!"

Jim shifted his weight, still not completely convinced. "They don't change the characters, do they?"

"A little, I guess," I replied. "But for the most part they are true to the original characters. You really can't mess with a classic. The characters are so relatable. I mean, you've got the Russian, the Scotsman, the African American, and the Asian. So no matter who you are, you've got someone you can relate to."

"Yeah, even if you're an alien like Spock," Jim laughed, a bit more relaxed.

Correcting him with my Trekkie-knowledge, I reminded him, "Come on now, Spock is only *half* alien."

We paid for our tickets and walked into the theater. I wanted to keep the conversation going, so I decided to try a little Talking Pictures.

"Actually, it's very defining of Spock's character that he's only half Vulcan alien. He's also half human, but he hates his humanity. He wishes he could be more logical and civilized like the Vulcans. But he's got a foot in both worlds." I paused and then added, "Kind of like us."

"Why?" he questioned. "How is that like us?"

Choosing my words very carefully, I responded, "We live in this world, but we're not *of* this world."

"I think you may be on science fiction overload," Jim said jokingly, punching my shoulder.

"Yeah, it may seem that way sometimes," I laughed.

We walked over to the snack counter and waited in line for the prerequisite bucket of popcorn. I glanced at my watch, realizing that the previews were already starting. I prayed silently that I could keep our conversation going a bit longer before we walked into the theater. "But seriously," I continued, "Even though we're living on this earth, I believe heaven is my home."

"Oh, that's right," Jim laughed again. "You're one of those perfect Christians. I always forget because you just seem so normal!"

"Thanks! But not even my mom thinks I'm normal!" I smiled as I pulled out my wallet for the cashier. Turning toward Jim, I added, "And *you* of all people should know that I'm not perfect! But actually, that brings me to another great point. Spock is a Vulcan and a human, and I'm a saint and a sinner. See? Two worlds coming together!"

"Saint and sinner?" He looked confused. "What do you mean?"

"I'm a sinner. I think and do things I shouldn't, and I don't do and think the good things that I should. But I believe that Jesus loves me so much that He died on the cross to forgive me of my sins. And because of Him, I am also a saint! Because when God looks at me, he doesn't see a sinner. He sees a saint loved and forgiven by Jesus. That's two worlds coming together for sure!"

I smiled at Jim as he pondered what I had just explained. I decided to let him think about it for awhile.

"Okay, let's go! We're missing the previews!" I exclaimed as we left the snack counter. "But seriously, think about Spock's two worlds while we watch this movie. It's a pretty interesting concept. And we can talk more about all this later." And armed with our popcorn and drinks, off we went into the theater.

Take 3

Redemptive Themes

Freedom and redemption are two of the more common themes found in movies. This is because they are also important themes in life. Regardless of faith or circumstances, we all have a deep longing and need to be forgiven, to be saved from the things that condemn us, and to experience the joy of freedom.

Freedom!

Throughout this book, I have purposely used a wide variety of examples from many movie genres instead of focusing on my own personal movie preferences. But now that's about to change. I'm excited to tell you that *Braveheart* is one of my all-time favorite movies. I have been tempted to quote it several times in this book, but I wanted to save it for this chapter on redemptive themes because it fits so perfectly here. Few movie scenes have ever touched my soul like the exclamation of "FREEDOM!" by William Wallace with his very last breath. He lived out the promise he made to his men (his "warrior-poets") when he first started the revolution: "They may take our lives, but they'll never take our freedom!" Ultimately, Wallace laid down his life for his countrymen. He refused to take the easy way out, even though it was presented to him by several different people, including his girlfriend. Even as a captive enemy of the state, he was free!

We all long for freedom from whatever entraps us. But interestingly enough, freedom always comes with sacrifice. Freedom isn't free – there is always a price – and yet freedom is absolutely priceless. As William Wallace said, "It's all for nothing if you don't have freedom." Our spiritual freedom cost Jesus His life, and He willingly gave it – no one took His life. God gave everything for your freedom!

Occasionally I'll hear people in the church talk about getting more "bang for our buck" when it comes to mission work. The issue I have with this terminology is that it sounds like we're putting a price tag on the human soul. Jesus put a price tag on the human soul... PRICELESS!

The parable of the Lost Sheep in Luke, chapter 15, affirms that Jesus loves each one of us individually as much as He loves all of us. The shepherd willingly left the 99 sheep that did not stray to go out and find the one that was lost. Why would he do that? He searched diligently because his love for each one of his flock was so great. This story is a powerful reminder that Jesus will go the extra mile to find and rescue each one of us. Even if you were the only person on the earth to ever sin and need a savior, Jesus would still have given His life, just for you! Why would He do that? He made the sacrifice because His love for each one of us is so great!

The Lost Sheep story is immediately followed by two other "lost" stories in Luke chapter 15: the Lost Coin and the Lost Son (sometimes called the Prodigal Son). While all three of the stories have a happy ending, it's interesting that Jesus chooses a coin, a sheep, and a son to illustrate His point. You see, the coin had no idea it was lost. It was just lost. And the owner rejoiced when it was found. The sheep unknowingly got lost. It just wandered off, as sheep often do. And the shepherd rejoiced when it was found. However, the third parable is a bit different. The son *chose* to get lost. The son knew the difference between right and wrong, but purposely chose the wrong path. He intentionally left. And still, when he realized his mistake and went back home, his father called for a huge party in his honor. They even went so far as to butcher the fattened calf. (Every great party needs some nice juicy steaks!) There was great rejoicing and celebrating, because what was lost was now found!

These parables illustrate that nothing gives God greater joy than when the lost is found. Jesus summed up His whole reason for coming to earth in Luke 19:10 – **"For the Son of Man came to seek and to save what was lost."** Note that Jesus isn't lost. People talk about "finding Jesus" in their lives, but they have it all backwards. We don't "find" Jesus. He finds *us*. We're the lost ones. Sometimes we don't know we're lost, like the coin. Sometimes we unintentionally wander off and get lost, like the sheep. And at other times, we flat out rebel and turn our backs on the Father. The story of the Prodigal Son is the story of you and me! But Jesus is always there to hold us, comfort us, and welcome us home. Remember that it doesn't matter how long we've been gone, or what has happened in the past. Jesus runs to meet us on the road, wraps His arms around us, and welcomes us home!

In the movie *Taken*, Liam Neeson plays a father searching for his 17-year-old daughter who was kidnapped while on a trip to Paris. He quickly learns that she will be sold as a slave unless he finds her in the next 96 hours. After all kinds of obstacles, struggles, and quite literal blood, sweat, and tears, he finally finds her. Overjoyed, she exclaims, "You came for me!"

"I told you I would," her loving father responds.

Our Heavenly Father has promised that he will always come for us as well. He loves and cares for us more than we can ever imagine. No matter what direction your life has taken, no matter what sinful behaviors seem to control you, Jesus is coming for you! We have One who fights valiantly for us.

It is fascinating how often we see redemptive themes in movies. Why is this so common? All of us need to be redeemed from something: the sins of our own making, the sins of our parents, the sins of our community/country, the sins of our enemies, or the sins that arise from simply living in a fallen world. The redemption stories in the movies we watch can provide us with a perfect opportunity to share with others the redemptive love of Jesus.

There is a seemingly insignificant scene in *High School Musical 3: Senior Year* that really resonated with me. It's where Troy Bolton, the local, hunky, basketball star, is taking off his basketball jersey for the very last time. There is no turning back; he is no longer a high school basketball player. I vividly remember taking off my high school jersey for the last time. It was an emotional moment, because it signified not only an ending but also a new beginning. It was time to move on to something else. Things would never be the same again. Something similar happens when Jesus comes into our lives. In 2 Corinthians 5:17 we are told: **"Therefore, if anyone is in Christ, he is a new creation; the old has gone, the new has come!"** Jesus longs to take the garment of sin off of our back, reclothe us in His righteousness and move us forward, never to look back at the chains of our past. That's redemption!

Redemption, freedom, forgiveness – these are some of the most common themes in movies because they are some of the most common themes in life. All people, believers and unbelievers alike, long to be redeemed, freed, and forgiven. My hope and prayer is that seeing those themes played out on the silver screen will increase your passion to see them in your life and in the lives of your friends and loved ones. Share the good news of our Savior Jesus Christ and the freedom He brings!

I've Been Redeemed

Have you seen your redemption story on the big screen? What movies contain themes of redemption and freedom that you can relate to? Do you know what your redemption story is? How has Jesus changed your life?

These are important questions. To understand redemption we first need to understand how Law and Gospel work together. God's pure and holy Law is our "S.O.S." – it Shows Our Sin. The Law reminds us that we are imperfect and fall short of what God expects of us. It shows us our helplessness and inability to rescue ourselves. It points to our absolute need for a savior. The Bible makes it clear that **"the wages of sin is death."** (Romans 6:23) We cannot save ourselves, and we deserve death and an eternity in hell. We *need* Jesus. This realization draws us to the Gospel message. The Gospel shows our Savior, Jesus, who is our Redeemer. By dying on the cross, He took the punishment we deserve. He conquered death by His resurrection, so we can live forever in our heavenly home with Him. Thanks be to God for such great love!

Once we recognize through the Law that we are sinners and are enlightened by the Gospel that we are saved by faith in Jesus, our response is sure to follow. We want to tell the whole world about Christ's life-changing love. Talking Pictures is a way we can share our gratitude for what Jesus has done for us.

Do you know what the most successful type of advertisement is for a movie? Think about it for a minute. Do you think it's a TV commercial? Website clip? Magazine or newspaper ad? Believe it or not, the best advertising method is simply what they call "word of mouth." It's the idea of someone enjoying a movie so much that they tell all of their friends to go see it. They loved the experience and want everyone to share in it.

Low-budget movies like *There's Something about Mary, My Big Fat Greek Wedding, Napoleon Dynamite*, and *Slumdog Millionaire* become megahits due to word-of-mouth advertising. Believe it or not, evangelism is word-of-mouth advertising too! It fits perfectly into our idea of Evangelist/ Translator. You've been redeemed and you can't help but tell the world about what you've experienced in a way they will understand. The excitement of redemption is contagious!

Have you ever noticed that there are several accounts in the Bible where, after healing someone, Jesus told the person not to tell anyone? This surprises us because we imagine that Jesus would have wanted everyone to know all about Him. Some think that Jesus said not to advertise certain miracles because He didn't want people to overreact – whether it be viewing Him only as a miracle-worker or seeking His death before His ministry was completed. However, when a life-changing experience happens, people simply can't keep silent. At the end of the miraculous story recorded in Mark chapter 7, we read: **"At this, the man's ears were opened, his tongue was loosened and he began to speak plainly. Jesus commanded them not to tell anyone. But the more he did so, the more they kept talking about it. People were overwhelmed with amazement."** (Mark 7:35-37) Do you catch the ancient Jerusalem word-of-mouth advertising going down in that story? The news spread like a wildfire! When you've been healed by Jesus, when you've experienced His love, you can't help but tell the world!

Another form of advertising that has been growing in popularity is called product placement. Instead of a movie star drinking a generic or fake brand of soda in the film, he or she is now drinking a Pepsi™. Many companies are paying big bucks to have their products featured in movies. They feel it's one of the best advertising methods. Notice that the star never says, "Drink Pepsi!" – he just drinks a Pepsi. He models it. He lives it out and influences us by his example. It reminds us that actions are more powerful than words. What do our actions say about our faith? Do we live it out and influence others by our example? An interesting quote that is often attributed to St. Francis of Assisi is: "Preach the Gospel at all times, and if necessary, use words." Our lives can speak volumes about who Jesus is and what redemption is, perhaps much louder than our words, and to a greater extent than we'll ever realize.

With his last dying breath, Tom Hanks says to Matt Damon's title character in *Saving Private Ryan*, "Earn this." Tom Hanks gave his life for Private Ryan. He didn't want Mrs. Ryan to have to lose another son in that dreadful world war. Private Ryan is later seen at a gravesite in tears because there is a tremendous pressure in "Earn this." Who could ever earn something of that magnitude? No one could live a life that can satisfy such a high standard. In an analogous way, none of us can satisfy the high standard set by God's Law. But Jesus did. He earned God's favor for us through His perfect life, death, and resurrection. We cannot do *one* thing to earn God's love or grace; it is a gift that we have been given. But we can be grateful, and can live out that gratitude in all that we say and do. We can live our lives for Jesus!

The B-I-B-L-E, Yes That's the Book for Me

Do you have a favorite Bible character? As a kid, mine was King David. I just loved the David and Goliath story. The idea that a young kid could take out a terrifying gargantuan warrior with one well-aimed rock from a slingshot absolutely fascinated me. He was a hero! As I've gotten older, however, I've realized that David's life was so much more than just the big showdown with the dreaded Philistine giant. He wasn't always a hero. Yes, David was chosen to be the next king even when he was still a very young boy. Yes, David was a talented musician and a dedicated shepherd. Yes, David was a man after God's own heart. But... David was also a big-time sinner. Adultery? CHECK! Envy? CHECK! Murder? CHECK! Somebody better call Brad Pitt and Morgan Freeman because we got another guy obsessed with the *Se7en* Deadly Sins!

All of our favorite characters from the Bible were far from perfect. Some of them, like Moses (who was unable to enter the earthly Promised Land), only received final redemption in death. But thankfully, for all who believe in Jesus Christ as Lord and Savior, death is not the end of the line. It is the glorious transformation into life eternal. I like to see tombstones that phrase the date of birth as "Entered life on...," and the date of death as "Entered eternal life on... ." This is a more accurate statement for Christians because death is far from the end – it's just another beginning! Forrest Gump may have been extremely wise, but his most famous saying – "Life was like a box of chocolates. You never know what you're gonna get" – just doesn't apply to the followers of Jesus. We know *exactly* what we're going to get, and we will receive it by God's grace. Heaven is our home, and Jesus is there right now preparing a place for us.

In *The Curious Case of Benjamin Button*, we see a man who lives life backwards. He's born as an old man and then "dies" when he becomes a little baby. The tag line for the movie, which is adapted from a famous quote by Soren Kierkegaard, reads: "Life can only be understood backward. It must be lived forward." Hindsight is 20/20, as they say, and it's always easier to see the right decisions and choices after the fact. (Ask anyone who's gambled in Vegas!) It's very easy to find ourselves wrestling with regrets and guilt over the things we've done or haven't done. But we know that no matter what we face on this earth, our eternal life is absolutely secure in Jesus. If we truly embrace that, we can live life with boldness and freedom, continually moving forward by God's grace.

Whether or not we believe in Jesus as our Savior, we are all going to enter into an eternal life. The question is this: Where are we going to spend our eternity? Will we be in heaven with our Lord Jesus and all of our brothers and sisters in Christ, or will we be in hell, where, as Jesus Himself describes it, **"there will be weeping and gnashing of teeth"** (Matthew 8:12)? I'm not exactly sure what "gnashing" of teeth is, but I'm positively sure that I don't want to experience it. I would venture to say that five out of five dentists would recommend not gnashing your teeth. Heaven is home to all who believe in Jesus Christ as Lord and Savior, and that salvation is found in Him alone. There is no other way!

As you can see, we have a very important role in sharing the love of Jesus with those who don't yet know Him. The truth of the matter is that all who do not believe in Jesus as their Lord and Savior – and yes, this just might include your coworkers, friends, parents, perhaps even your spouse or children – will spend their eternities in hell. Does that statement make you cringe? I hope it does! God wants you to be concerned about the eternity of others. Hell isn't pretty to talk about, and nowadays it's even considered politically incorrect! To make themselves feel better, some Christians even say that there *is* no hell. But make no mistake, hell is very, *very* real. I'm not bringing all this up to scare you. I'm reminding you about it because it is a very serious reality. As believers in Jesus, we know that heaven is our home. And as Dorothy reminds us in *The Wizard of Oz:* "There's no place like home!" We have nothing to fear. But others do. We should do what we can, by the power of the Holy Spirit, to be sure all of our loved ones will be coming home to heaven with us. Jesus is in heaven right now preparing a place for us, and it is His desire that our friends and family will share in eternal life with Him! Jesus is the only one who can truly say, "I'm the king of the world!" (I just had to work a *Titanic* quote in this book somewhere! It's one of the biggest movies of all time!)

The American Film Institute (AFI) recently made a list of the 100 greatest movie quotes of all time. They ranked the line, "Frankly my dear, I don't give a damn" from *Gone with the Wind* as #1. Ironic, isn't it? That line is exactly the *opposite* of what Talking Pictures is all about. We *do* care! We don't want anyone to be damned, and to end up in hell. And because we care, we can't help but tell those around us about Jesus and his love.

The theme of redemption can be found throughout the Bible. Whether clinging to a redemptive promise or a re-demptive person (Jesus), the Bible is filled with sinful people like you and me – people who are in need of a Savior. Next time you are watching a movie, be looking for a redemptive storyline that can be related to a Bible story. For example, maybe there is a revenge theme in the movie. Do you recall any revenge themes in the Bible? What about the story of Jacob and Esau? With Esau intent on retaliation, Jacob had to flee for his life (Genesis 27:41-43). That's something we've seen in quite a few movies. How did revenge play out in the Esther story? Haman was determined to get even with the Jews (Esther 3). He had the horrid idea of ridding the world of the Jewish race a few thousand years before Hitler.

The Bible is filled with the same themes that are found in the biggest Hollywood blockbusters. Jason Bourne was betrayed and abandoned by his country in the *Bourne* movie series. But no one has experienced the betrayal of a friend quite like Jesus did with Judas (Luke 22:47-48). And it didn't end there. After being betrayed, Jesus then endured the denial of Peter, who was one of His closest friends (Luke 22:54-61). Hasn't Jack Sparrow betrayed his friends a few times to save his own behind in *The Pirates of the Caribbean* movies? Jack unconvincingly tells us in *Pirates of the Caribbean: Dead Man's Chest*, "You can mistrust me less than you can mistrust him. Trust me." Of course the audience knows that until the credits role, Jack cannot be trusted at all. Betrayal and deceit are themes that are commonly found in popular movies, and there are plenty of opportunities to relate a movie character's situation back to a Biblical story.

You've Been Redeemed

If your friend or relative doesn't yet know Jesus, have they really ever experienced true forgiveness? If they don't know the love of Christ, have they ever experienced true, genuine love? These are important and difficult questions.

We all need redemption, and I believe that deep down we all realize this because St. Paul reminds us in the book of Romans that God's Law is written on our hearts (Romans 2:15). However, not everyone knows where to find it. We know we need help, but so many are looking for it on the wrong path. Too many people seek comfort in the sinful pleasures and ways of this world. Others look for some kind of salvation within themselves, believing that they can do it all on their own. But as Christians, where does *our* help come from? Where can we find shelter from the storms of life? When looking for answers to some of life's biggest questions, I love to turn to the book of Psalms. The Psalms were written by people who struggled with the same things you and I struggle with. The writer of Psalm 91 has some very reassuring words for us in the first two verses: **"He who dwells in the shelter of the Most High will rest in the shadow of the Almighty. I will say of the LORD, 'He is my refuge and my fortress, my God, in whom I trust.'"** (Psalm 91:1-2) A mighty fortress is our God! He is our shelter. He is our sanctuary. In *The Sixth Sense*, when Haley Joel Osment was "seeing dead people," where did he go to escape? He went to the sanctuary. He felt safe in God's house – in His sanctuary. God is our refuge from the pain and struggles of this earth, and the one true path to everlasting life.

I've seen a very disturbing trend in a few movies such as *The Devil's Advocate, End of Days*, and *Constantine*. All of these movies deal with the topic of spiritual warfare, good *vs.* evil, with a manifestation of Satan. But in all of these films, they portray that the only way the "hero" can defeat Satan is through suicide – through quitting and giving up. In *The Devil's Advocate*, Keanu Reeves even says, "Free will, right?" before he laughs and shoots himself in the head. This is *not* how Satan is defeated!

Reread the story of Judas's last few hours in Matthew chapter 27. Sadly, Judas committed suicide because it was the only thing he could think of to do. He tried going to the religious leaders for forgiveness, confessing his sin in betraying Jesus. He knew that he had betrayed innocent blood, but the only response he received was: **"What is that to us? That's your responsibility."** (Matthew 27:4) The Church is the place where one receives God's abundant grace and forgiveness. Unfortunately for Judas, the religious leaders he went to were not part of the true fellowship of believers. What was Judas to do? Unfortunately, he lost all hope and took his own life.

After Peter denied knowing Jesus – not once, not twice, but three times – he **"wept bitterly."** (Luke 22:54-62) But Peter still had hope that Jesus would prevail. Peter didn't give up! He was embarrassed and regretted his shameful behavior, but he still put his life in the hands of Jesus. Peter is indeed restored by Jesus, as we read in John 21:15-19.

Satan has been defeated by the blood of Christ. I sometimes wonder if the reason some of these movies portray the hero committing suicide is because they actually view

Christ's act as a suicide. But what Jesus did was *not* suicide; it was *sacrifice*. There is a world of difference! Jesus willingly laid down His life for the purpose of rescuing you and me from the death we deserve because of our sins. Satan has no power over us! Make no mistake – Satan is real and he wants to destroy you. But Jesus has redeemed you! You are His for all eternity.

Redemption needs to be experienced. As Christopher McCandless says in *Into The Wild*: "God's place is all around us. It is in everything and in anything we can experience. People just need to change the way they look at things." The redemptive experience is the grand finale, the closing act, of Talking Pictures. In our conversations with our friends who don't know Jesus, let's look for opportunities to bring out redemptive themes in movies in ways they can understand and relate to. Discussions about redemptive themes naturally point to Jesus.

Pray about It

- Thank God for His redemption and ask Him to enable you to experience this in new and profound ways.

Talk about It

- How do you define redemption? Forgiveness? Freedom? Love? Would a follower of Jesus and someone who doesn't believe have the same definitions? Why or why not?

- What movies have themes that strongly speak of redemption to you? Forgiveness? Freedom? Unconditional love?

- Which flawed, sinful, ordinary character from the Bible do you identify with the most? Why?

- What are some specific ways you can use word-of-mouth advertising to share your faith with others?

Live It Out

- Think of a time in your life when you were the lost sheep in Jesus' parable. What lured you away from the fold? How did Jesus bring you back? Or perhaps you see yourself more clearly in the story of the Prodigal Son. What was the turning point when you realized you wanted to come back home? Think about such details of your story and how you can share them with others who may be wandering sheep (or defiant sons) right now. Write it down if it helps you to compose your thoughts more effectively. Who do you know that would greatly benefit from hearing your story?

Talking Pictures Example #8

As we left the movie theater, I was more than a little pumped from the visual adrenaline we'd just experienced on the silver screen. *"Transformers: Revenge of the Fallen!"* I shouted in a robotic voice.

"I'm surprised it actually took them this long to make another *Transformers* movie," Tim said sarcastically.

"Don't be negative! It was a fun movie," I insisted.

"The only thing I'm negative about is that they now make *Transformers* toys that don't transform. They're just robots!" he complained. "A transformer is supposed to transform!"

"Good point," I conceded. "That doesn't make sense. Why would a transformer not transform?"

"See? If the movies were better," Tim reasoned, "the toys would be better too!"

"Interesting argument," I laughed. Seeing that he was serious, I added, "It's frustrating when something is supposed to act in a certain way and it doesn't."

"Thank you," he said, feeling somewhat vindicated.

"In fact, I think that's how God feels about us," I said. I knew that Tim wasn't a Christian, and I had always hoped for an opportunity to share my faith with him. I wasn't sure how he would respond, but I had already decided that this was the evening that I was going to try to work it into the conversation.

After a short silence, Tim looked at me inquisitively. "Huh?"

"God made us to be transformed." Oops – that wasn't quite what I had intended to say. "No, wait, let me explain that better. God made us *perfect* – in His image, in fact. But we were the ones who sinned and screwed things up, and now we need Him to change us back into His image." I paused for a moment, and then added, "God transforms us."

Thinking for a moment, he asked, "God does *what?*"

"He *transforms* us," I replied emphatically. "God changes us. He moves in us, and flows through us." I began to pray silently that God would work through this conversation.

"Whoa! Now you're sounding like Obi-Wan Kenobi," Tim laughed.

I laughed in agreement. "Yeah, maybe you're right about that!"

We crossed the street and walked briskly, heading back toward campus. I decided to try to continue the conversation. "Here's something I've been thinking about: God loves us just the way we are, but He loves us too much to keep us that way. God has a transformation in mind for us. That's why He sent us His Son Jesus." I paused for a moment, and then continued. "When Jesus comes into our lives, everything changes. No matter what we've done or how badly we've screwed things up, we are forgiven and restored. Jesus works in our hearts and makes everything new." There – I had done it. I had used the name of Jesus.

As we walked along for the next few blocks, Tim was completely silent. I had expected him to make a joke about what I had said, or even disagree with me. I knew his personality, and I was ready for his teasing or arguing. I knew I could give it right back to him and still get my point across. But I wasn't prepared for him to say nothing at all. This wasn't the Tim I knew. I began to worry that maybe I had played too many cards, too fast. I sweated and prayed to myself, waiting for him to respond. I finally understood the meaning of the expression "deafening silence."

As we approached an intersection and waited for the light to change, Tim suddenly turned toward me. He looked rattled and scared. "Okay, man, who told you?" he demanded.

I was completely confused. "What?"

"Somebody told you about what's been going on, right?" His voice wavered a bit, changing from anger to embarrassment. "I mean, what I've been involved in the past few months."

"Nobody told me anything, really!" I insisted. "I'm really clueless here, man. I honestly have no idea what you're talking about."

He swallowed hard and kicked at the curb, trying to find the right words. "Well…," he started, and then hesitated. The light changed and we walked on down the street. I waited patiently for him to gather his words and his courage. Finally he continued. "Well, I've kinda screwed up some stuff in my life lately. It's pretty bad. When you were saying all that stuff about changing – well – I need to do some transforming myself. But I don't know how."

I knew that God had just opened the door for a much deeper conversation than I had ever expected. "Well, for starters," I said, "let's stop and pray right now… ."

Keep It Rolling

In the final chapter (so far) of the *Die Hard* saga, *Live Free or Die Hard*, Bruce Willis's most famous character, John McClane, unveils a stunning confession. Although he has already saved the world three times, he admits that he really doesn't want to be a hero. This is how he explains it: "You know what you get for being a hero? Nothin'. You get shot at. You get a little pat on the back, blah, blah, blah, attaboy. You get divorced. Your wife can't remember your last name. Your kids don't want to talk to you. You get to eat a lot of meals by yourself. Trust me, kid, nobody wants to be that guy." John McClane would much rather let someone else be the hero. But, since no one else is rising up and taking action, he's got to do it! He doesn't have a choice. He's compelled to do what he's called to do.

In our lives as Christians, we too are called to be a people of action. God wants you to be a hero – an Evangelist/ Translator! With God there are no coincidences. He's always got a plan. There is no such thing as being in the wrong place at the wrong time, because He will always work through your circumstances. God will use you right where you are – wherever you happen to be!

Maybe you've never thought of yourself as an Evangelist/Translator before, and it scares you a little (or a lot!). Don't ever let fear stop you from doing something God has called you to do! As Yoda says in *Star Wars: Episode I – The Phantom Menace*, "Fear is the path to the dark side."

Maybe you took the "spiritual gifts test" and you didn't score very high in the gift of evangelism section.

Perhaps you're not sure about the translator part either. But we all can witness, and we all can speak to how a shared experience (for example, a movie) relates to our spiritual life. Talking Pictures is about God working within us, through the unique gifts and resources He has already given us. You can do something easy and simple, like taking a friend to a movie. You can share your own ideas and life experiences, and open the door for a deeper spiritual connection. Start small, and trust that God will work through all of these opportunities – and that He will give you more as you are ready. Don't worry about the things you *can't* do. Focus instead on what you *can* do, and believe that Jesus will do it through you! Philippians 4:13 sums it up well: **"I can do everything through him who gives me strength."**

Let's think about that verse for a minute. Do you know what "I can do everything" really means? That's a powerful statement! Does it mean that you could become the Queen of England? Does it mean you could become a mermaid? Does it mean you could jump off the Empire State Building and fly, or survive 6 months without eating? Of course not. What it *does* mean is you can do everything God has called you to do. God has given you all the strength and resources you need to do everything He wants you to accomplish. Also remember that God never gives us more than we can handle (1 Corinthians 10:13). He pushes us and stretches us, molds us and shapes us, so we are always growing and changing. But He does not overburden us. He equips us with all the talents, means and opportunities we need to serve Him and tell others about His love.

Gifts and Gadgets for His Glory

In the movie remake of the classic TV show, *Get Smart*, Steve Carrell's character uses his unique skills and all kinds of clever gizmos to save the day. He isn't as physically strong as the other agents, and he certainly isn't as smart or experienced. And perhaps most importantly in the spy film genre, he isn't as good-looking as the other agents. But he uses his gifts and some very clever gadgets – like the shoe phone, a tooth two-way radio, and a "spy fly," among others – to the best of his ability. And in using his natural skills and available tools, he eventually saves the day.

God wants us to glorify Him in all that we do – in our work, in our play, in our worship, and in every relationship. That sounds like a tall order, but He has uniquely equipped each one of us with our own set of talents, abilities, and resources. Through these "gifts and gadgets," we are able to share our faith with those around us.

Do you know which gifts God has given you? How are you using them? Do you know the difference between gifts and passions? In the movie *Napoleon Dynamite*, when Pedro was wondering about his own gifts, Napoleon told him: "Well, you have a sweet bike. And you're really good at hooking up with chicks. Plus you're like the only guy at school who has a mustache." All wonderful skills to be sure, but to really succeed and get the most joy out of life, one needs to find ways to connect their gifts and passions. Gifts are similar to skills – these are the natural, God-given abilities that we possess. Passions are the things you love, and that you dream about being and doing.

Music is a great example of this. There are millions of wannabe rock stars out there. And Guitar Hero and Rock Band video games have just added to the obsession. Musical ability is a gift. My mom is a professional musician, while my dad can't sing at all. Growing up, no one wanted to sit next to Dad in church because he sang loud and off pitch, and it was painful to listen to. So while music is a gift, music is also a great passion for many people. Passion can sometimes be an ungifted love. Look at many of the people who try out for

American Idol. They can't sing, they have no musical gifted-ness, but they certainly have a passion for music. Those who have both the gift and the passion for music are the ones who can really become rock stars! Do you know what your gifts are?

Do you possess any "gadgets" that can be used to help spread the Gospel? Movies could be one of your gadgets. What other technology could be a gadget for you to use to share the love of Jesus? What about your cell phone? Cell phones are one of the fastest growing technologies in the history of the world. How did we ever survive before cell phones? We use them constantly. How can you use this life-changing gadget to change lives for Jesus? Maybe change your ring tone to a Christian song, or text your friend words of encouragement, Scripture, or simply "I'm praying for you."

Martin Luther used the gadget of the printing press. Billy Graham used the gadget of television and radio. Underground, illegal Christian churches who are suffering persecution all over the world are using the gadget of the Internet to stay connected and educated. How can you use the latest technological gadgets to God's glory and advance His Kingdom?

Keep Your Eye on the Ball

Recently, I've been playing a lot of baseball in the backyard with my two young daughters. After every pitch I make, I find myself saying, "Keep your eye on the ball." It's an involuntary reflex. I can't help it. It just comes out. I've been tempted to say, "There's no crying in baseball!" like Tom Hanks's character in *A League of Their Own*, but so far I've been able to restrain myself.

My dad always told me to keep my eye on the ball when we would play ball in the back yard. I'm sure his dad had told him the same thing, and so on. In order to hit the ball, you can't lose focus. Staying focused means eliminating distractions, tuning out what's unimportant, and concentrating completely on the task at hand.

In the movie *For Love of the Game*, Kevin Costner's character is a baseball player (once again) but this time he is in the twilight of his Hall of Fame career, looking for one more moment of glory. The movie centers on him throwing a perfect game, while experiencing flashbacks upon his life. This is a high-pressure, nerve-wracking situation. But the character's strength is his sharp focus. All he needs to do is to say to himself, "Turn on the mechanism," and he no longer hears the crowds, the opposing team, or any of the stadium noise. In his mind, he's just playing a little game of catch, just as he's done a thousand times before. That's what true focus is all about – simplifying a complicated task into its most basic form. He's not throwing a perfect game in the final game of the season and perhaps of his career; he's just playing catch.

If the idea of sharing your faith seems overwhelming, try to keep your focus on what is really at the heart of it all. Don't think about it as evangelism. Instead, focus on simply talking to people about Jesus, your friend and brother – just as naturally and comfortably as you would talk about any of the important people in your life. Keep your focus on Jesus, and don't allow the distractions, fears, and doubts of the world to throw you off course.

The author of the book of Hebrews says: **"Let us fix our eyes on Jesus, the author and perfecter of our faith."** (Hebrews 12:2) In other words, we need to keep our eye on the ball. We need to keep our hearts and minds centered on Christ so we can point the way for others. Talking Pictures is about bringing people to Jesus and letting *Him* do the work.

All we need to do is have Jesus be the focus of our inter-
actions with others. St. Paul, arguably the greatest evangelist
of all time, tells us: **"For I resolved to know nothing while I
was with you except Jesus Christ and him crucified."** (1
Corinthians 2:2) It's all about Jesus – His life, death, and resurrection.

People who encounter Jesus are changed. It's funny
how things that were once so important to us tend to lose their
significance once Jesus comes into our lives. Priorities
change dramatically. St. Paul says that we become new
creations when we get connected to Jesus (2 Corinthians
5:17). As I mentioned earlier in the book, folks I've known
who have overcome addictions all reached a point during
their recovery when they realized they needed to stop
associating with certain people. When someone meets Jesus,
they cast away the bad influences that they really needed to
lose all along. And by His power, those distractions aren't
missed. God fills us up with those things which are of eternal
value! Like Hiccup says in *How to Train Your Dragon*,
"Everything we know about you guys (dragons) is wrong!"
When you encounter Jesus, you find that everything you
thought you knew about the world was dead wrong.

A good example of a person's priorities being
radically shifted after an encounter with Jesus is found in
John 4:4-30. There we find a Samaritan woman who meets
Jesus, seemingly by chance (but we know better), and their
short conversation changes her life. The last few verses have
always stood out to me: **"Then, leaving her water jar, the
woman went back to the town and said to the people,
'Come, see a man who told me everything I ever did.
Could this be the Christ?' They came out of the town and
made their way toward him."** (John 4:28-30)

Three significant things happened as a result of this
woman's meeting with Jesus. First, she left behind her water
jar. Filling that jar was her whole purpose in being at the well

in the first place! But once she encountered Jesus, she was so excited to share the news that she totally forgot about the jar. Our purpose and priorities change when Jesus enters our life.

Next, after encountering Jesus she told everyone in town to come and see Him. She didn't fully understand what had happened at the well. She didn't have all the answers. She didn't suddenly become a perfect human being. But she *did* know that something had just happened that would change her life forever. She was excited, joyful, and filled with hope. In her enthusiasm, she went and told everyone who would listen. When we come to faith, our natural response is to talk about Jesus and share Him with others.

Finally, other people made their way to meet Jesus because of her testimony. The woman didn't have to drag everyone down to the well with her. Her focus was on Jesus, and she simply directed them to Him. People instantly saw the change in her and wanted to see this Jesus with their own eyes. When others see us experiencing Jesus and the life-changing effect He has, they will want to check it out!

Let's go back for a moment to the baseball movie *For Love of the Game.* Kevin Costner is the pitcher, but he's not alone out there on the field. He's got a whole diamond full of teammates behind him and supporting him. His catcher reminds him of this: "The boys are all here for ya, we'll back you up, we'll be there, cause, Billy, we don't stink right now. We're the best team in baseball, right now, right this minute, because of you. You're the reason. We're not gonna screw that up, we're gonna be awesome for you right now. Just throw." We, too, can rely on our teammates – our fellow brothers and sisters in Christ. Other believers can help us and encourage us to be confident witnesses to our friends, and through it all stay focused on Jesus. Remember, it's not good for man to be alone! Find prayer partners, accountability partners, good friends, and a solid church family who will all encourage you in your role as Evangelist/Translator.

Remember that it is all about Jesus – not about us, or how skilled we are in our witnessing efforts. We merely point the way; we aren't the way. Keep your eyes focused on Jesus, the only Way, Truth and Life (John 14:6).

Keep Praying

There is a powerful scene in the movie *We Were Soldiers*, where before heading into battle – a brutal battle where both sides knew many lives would be lost – Mel Gibson and the leader of the Vietnamese army are both seen praying in their separate churches. They have no idea that the other is also praying at the very same moment. They are actually praying for the very same things. Both are earnest in their prayers and prayer rituals. But only one is praying to God the Father, Son, and Holy Spirit. Prayer is more than meditation or clearing your mind. Prayer is connecting with the God of the Universe!

Always remember the tremendous power of prayer. Prayer is our phone line to the heart of God, and He should be #1 on our speed dial! I find it interesting that as a society, we place such a high value on communication that we never go anywhere without our cell phones and ready access to our e-mail. And yet we are surprisingly slow at times to tap into our easiest and most powerful communication tool of all – talking to God in prayer.

God does hear every single prayer, and He does answer every one. Of course He doesn't always answer with a "yes." Sometimes God has to tell us "no," like any loving parent. The Father told Jesus "no" in the Garden of Gethsemane when Jesus asked if there was another way to redeem the world other than dying on the cross. Sometimes God says "wait," as in 1 Chronicles 28:2-6 when King David wanted to build a temple. God told him it wasn't the right time. We may have to do some growing and maturing in our faith before we're really ready to receive what it is we're praying for. Prayer is always our power source, even when it's not answered in the way we want it to be.

We can't save anyone. We can't change anyone. We can't open the human heart. But prayer can! Prayer is the path that connects us to the very heart of God, who works miracles every day. Jesus modeled prayer for us throughout His life. He frequently went away by Himself to pray. If the perfect and Holy Son of God felt the need to pray so often, then we – as flawed, sinful humans – need it even more!

Another way that Jesus demonstrates the importance of prayer is when He got angry with the money changers in the temple (Matthew 21:12-13). Everyone likes to focus on how Jesus got upset and kicked out the "bad guys" (and by the way, notice that He didn't just kick out the sellers – He also kicked out the buyers!). But notice what Jesus says in verse 13: **"My house will be called a house of prayer."** Jesus was angry because prayer was not the priority.

Shortly after the story of the money changers, we come across Jesus withering a fig tree. This is another one of those stories where people like to focus on Jesus getting angry. He cursed a fig tree for not fulfilling its purpose, and it shriveled up and died (Matthew 21:18-22). The disciples were amazed. They had seen Jesus walk on water, raise the dead, and feed thousands of people – yet withering the fig tree really astounded them. Again, it's easy to focus on the anger exhibited in the story, but the point of the story goes back to prayer. Jesus closes the fig tree encounter with these words: **"If you believe, you will receive whatever you ask for in prayer."** (Matthew 21:22)

The interesting thing about prayer is that Jesus says our Heavenly Father already knows what we need before we even ask (Matthew 6:32). And yet He still wants us to come to Him in prayer with everything – all the big stuff, all the small stuff, and everything in between. If He already knows what we need even before we ask, why do we need to pray? We pray because it builds and strengthens the relationship we have with God. In any relationship, communication is a key factor impacting success or failure. Almost every time I've provided family-counseling – whether it be for a husband and wife, a parent and child, or siblings – communication was significantly lacking in the relationship. Communication (both speaking *and* listening) is the key to a healthy relationship. God desires a strong and healthy relationship with us. Even though He already knows the desires of our heart, He still longs to connect with us in prayer. I actually like how Ricky Bobby prays in *Talladega Nights*. I'm sure it offended some people when he prayed to "Lord baby Jesus," but to me it showed a desire for an intimate relationship. God wants an intimate relationship with us in prayer – not a programmed response!

God wants to listen, but He also wants to speak. That's right! Prayer isn't just about us reciting our wish list to God, like putting in our order at a drive-through window. Prayer is also about listening to the voice of God. He wants you to hear His plans and dreams for you.

When I talk to people about the concept of listening to God, many of them ask me what the voice of God sounds like. It's a great question, and everyone wants to know the answer. What does the voice of God sound like? Human beings have been wondering that since we were kicked out of the Garden of Eden after the Fall. In the Garden, the voice of God had been crystal clear. Adam and Eve had known exactly what God's voice sounded like. But since then, part of the mystery and journey of faith has been to discern God's voice. Sure, Moses had his burning bush (Exodus 3:2-4), and Elijah had his small still voice (1 Kings 19:11-13). People often tell me that God has told them to do something – apply for a particular job, start a family, or perhaps call someone they haven't thought of in twenty years. Occasionally I even have folks claim that God told them that *I* should do something! Did you know that in the classic movie *The Ten Commandments*, Charleton Heston not only plays Moses but also the voice of God? Sometimes I think this is our problem as well. We hear our own voice and think it is God's. How do we know with certainty that what we are hearing is God's voice?

      The bottom line is that God speaks to everyone differently. Actually, I'm very thankful for that because I'm not sure how I would handle a burning bush! To test whether it is God speaking to you, ask if the message is aligned with Scripture. For example, that's not God's voice telling you that it's okay to have sex with your boyfriend. Rather, God speaks to us in everything that is consistent with the teachings of the Bible.

      For me, God has always spoken by placing seemingly crazy, illogical and all-consuming ideas into my brain – the kind of ideas that make no sense and that are sure to bring raised eyebrows and maybe even ridicule from others. *Offer that drunk a ride home. Give that homeless person the food you just bought for yourself. Tell that complete stranger that you're praying for them.* Logic (and society) tell us not to get involved. Logic says, *Don't approach that destitute guy talking to himself – he's crazy! Don't give that lady a handout or you'll just enable her dependence on others. Don't stop for that mother crying at the train station – you'll be late for your meeting. Just worry about your own problems; look out for yourself! These people must be in their bad situation for a reason, so they need to learn their lesson the hard way. Don't talk to strangers! It's not safe.*

      The problem with logic is that it's human logic. God doesn't always work in a way that seems sensible to the world. God's logic is so far above our understanding. Even God's love is so illogical. Think about it. He loves sinners.

Sinners! He loves us even though we are constantly rebelling against Him. What's more, God sacrificed His own Son – who was perfect and without sin – to save a world full of rebellious screwups. We can't fully comprehend the logic of this because it's not how things work in human terms. In our world, fairness dictates that the good are rewarded and the bad are punished. **"Very rarely will anyone die for a righteous man, though for a good man someone might possibly dare to die. But God demonstrates his own love for us in this: While we were still sinners, Christ died for us."** (Romans 5:7-8) His "illogical love" calls *us* to be illogical too, and to love the unlovable.

So, how does God speak to you? Through the Bible? Through your Christian friends? Through an inspirational hymn or praise song? Through the smile of a child? Through the beauty of creation? Through a voice in your head, or maybe a "crazy" idea in your heart? Perhaps the most important thing we can do in connecting to Jesus, both in prayer and in life, is simply to listen and love. Don't complain about how God chooses to talk to you. Just be thankful that He does! We tend to think of prayer as us doing all the talking, but listening is every bit as important in our prayer relationship with God.

I want to share with you a memory verse. This verse can change your life. It's one of the very shortest verses in all of Scripture, but it's so vital to who we are as Christians. Even if your memory is bad, I guarantee you can memorize it. Ready? Look up 1 Thessalonians 5:17. Highlight it. Underline it. Print it out on your computer and tape it to your bathroom mirror. Do whatever you need to do to make sure you never forget it. For those of you who don't have your Bible handy, it says: **"pray continually."** That's it. Those two words are packed with power. They sum up a life of faith as well as anything. We need to be in constant communication with God – speaking and listening in all aspects of prayer: praising Him, thanking Him, confessing, seeking Him, connecting, asking, lifting up concerns. All of it is prayer, and it's a blessed gift and privilege!

Nehemiah was a man who greatly valued prayer. He had been chosen by God to rebuild the walls in Jerusalem following the exile. Nehemiah understood that when the going gets tough, the tough get praying! While several of his prayers are recorded in the book of Nehemiah, there is one seemingly insignificant verse that gives us a powerful example of how we are to pray: **"we prayed to our God and posted a guard day and night to meet this threat."** (Nehemiah 4:9) You see, even when things were dire and enemies threatened their very existence, what did they do? They prayed and they "posted."

They prayed that God would protect them. They prayed that God would bless their efforts, and strengthen them. They prayed that God would work for good. But note that they didn't just stop at prayer. The Bible says that they also "posted." Even though they prayed for protection, they still used the brains that God had given them and posted a guard for protection. They prayed and they posted. They expected God to work, and they worked as well.

Have you ever prayed to do well on a test, but didn't study? Have you ever prayed to make new friends, but then forgot to be friendly? Have you ever prayed for a promotion at work, but didn't put in your best effort to deserve it? God doesn't want us to pray for something and then plop on the couch, watch TV, and lazily wait for Him to do His stuff. God wants us to use the brain and gifts He blessed us with. The order is important, however. Remember: pray and *then* post. Through our prayers, God will give us the strength to be constantly posting.

Our friends who do not yet know Jesus will only come into knowledge of Him through our praying and posting. Pray that God will open their hearts and minds. Pray that God will change their lives. Pray that God will bring them into eternal life. And pray that God will use you in your role as Evangelist/Translator!

Cut! That's a Wrap!

Are you ready to be an Evangelist/Translator? Are you ready for an adventure that is greater than any action movie? Are you ready to share a love that is far above that of any sweeping romantic epic? The situation at hand is more serious than the most suspenseful drama. There are times it will be more mind-bending than any science fiction or fantasy.

In Hebrews 11:23, we are told that Moses' parents protected him from the mass slaughter of Hebrew babies, **"because they saw he was no ordinary child."** Well, my friends, guess what? *You, too,* are no ordinary child! There is no such thing as an ordinary child. Each one of us has more God-given potential then we will ever come close to realizing. I'm praying that you will become the very dream that Jesus has for you, because you are no ordinary child. You are *God's* child!

You may not know all the mysteries of God – none of us do. But He's not looking for ability. He's looking for *availability*. Are you available to see God at work in you? Are you open to all He has in store for you? It's going to be fun. Grab a friend, a movie, and some popcorn, and watch God at work! And remember what Maximus says in the movie *Gladiator*: "What we do in life echoes in eternity." It's showtime!

Pray about It

- Pray that God will use you as His Evangelist/Translator!

Talk about It

- What are your gifts? Have you ever taken a spiritual gifts inventory? How can you use your talents to glorify God?

- What things in your life should you leave behind so you can better focus on Jesus?

- In Matthew 6:32, Jesus says that our Heavenly Father already knows what we need before we ask. Why, then, should we still come to God in prayer?

- Think of some of your recently answered prayers. Which ones were answered with a "yes?" Which were answered with a "no" or "wait?" Do you see any patterns in God's answers to your requests? Why do you think God said "no" or "wait" in some of those circumstances?

- What are some specific ways you can help your non-Christian friends by praying and "posting?"

Live It Out

- Reflect on the occasions when you brought the first two friends on your list from the beginning of this book to see a movie. Was it easy to initiate a spiritual discussion with them afterward? What aspects of the discussion were the easiest? What parts were more difficult? What would you do differently next time?

It's time to invite the third friend on your list to come see a movie with you. Use the ideas and examples in this book as an inspiration and encouragement. Above all, pray for your friend and for opportune moments to share the miraculous message of the Gospel.

- Lastly, don't put this book on a shelf and forget about it. Share it with other Christian friends and family members, and find ways to encourage and support one another in your evangelism efforts.

Talking Pictures Example #9

As we were flipping through the channels late at night, we stumbled upon *Titanic*. "I can't believe *Titanic* was ranked the biggest movie ever for twelve years straight," remarked my friend Dan, groaning.

"Why not?" I asked. "It's got everything: action, romance, adventure, disaster, and mystery. It's a powerful story."

"I guess," Dan shrugged, leaning back in his chair, "but it all just seems kinda cheesy."

"No, it's not," I assured him. "It's something we can all connect with. It's a redemption story."

"What redemption story?" Dan seemed a bit annoyed. "It's a disaster story! There's no happy ending. The boat sinks and tons of people are killed. Jack dies, and Rose loses her one true love and has to start a whole new life."

"That's exactly it!" I said, excitedly. Dan looked confused, so I continued. "Jack sacrifices his life to save Rose. Rose was trapped in a life that she didn't want. She was pressured by her parents and her fiancé to live a life that was a lie, and Jack saved her. He helped her to see just how big the world is. Jack helped to set her free."

"He set her free from a world of riches and high-class living," he scoffed. "Oh, *poor* Rose!"

"Well," I said, "but she was miserable. She couldn't be herself and just do the things she wanted to do. She couldn't marry anyone she wanted. What kind of life is that?" I paused to turn down the volume on the TV. "What good is it for a person to gain the whole world, but lose his own soul?"

"What's that mean? Sounds like some famous quote or something." Dan grabbed a handful of pretzels from the bag beside him.

"Actually, yes," I explained. "It's a famous quote from the Bible. It means that money isn't everything. You could have all the money and possessions in the world, but they're not worth anything if you lose your own soul in the process."

"Well, maybe money can't buy everything, but it sure can buy a lot!" he insisted.

"Money can buy a lot of *stuff*," I conceded, "but then what? What really matters? Like the Beatles said, it can't buy me love."

"Can't buy me love! Ain't that the truth!" Dan laughed. "I think we've all tried that one before." He smiled to himself, remembering some of his past relationship blunders.

"Money can't buy what's really important in life," I continued. It can't buy respect – at least not genuine respect. It can't buy good, close friends. It can't buy us self-esteem or happiness or contentment."

"Yeah, okay, you've got something there," Dan admitted. "It's true that none of those things can be bought." I decided to continue a bit deeper with my point. "It also can't buy us freedom from our own mistakes, sins, and screwups."

"Well, there's *no way* we can ever be free of our past mistakes. We're stuck with those. Nothing will make those go away. Believe me, I've tried." Dan sighed, pushing away the bag of pretzels. "There's a lot of stuff I wish I hadn't done, you know? Lots of people I've hurt. Lots of decisions I've made that turned out bad." He paused for a moment, looking dejected. "I'd give anything to be free of all the stuff I've done wrong in my life."

What would your response be to Dan?

"Reeling" Them In

"Come, follow me," Jesus said, "and I will make you fishers of men." (Matthew 4:19)

The concept of being a "fisher of men" has always intrigued me. You see, I've never really had the patience to be a very good fisherman. When I was a kid, I always imagined fishing to be a lot more fun than it really was. I expected to drop a line into the water and then just pull out one fish after another. I assumed that all you had to do was show up, and the fish would practically jump into the boat by themselves. But in reality, fishing requires a great deal of patience. I would get antsy waiting for what seemed like an eternity for the fish to finally take the bait. It's easy to get bored after awhile and give up when nothing seems to be happening. Of course it's exciting when you finally get a tug on the line, but reeling it in requires skill and even more patience. If you're not careful, you'll lose what you waited so long to achieve.

And now we've come to the point where we need to address the next step in our vocation as Evangelist/Translator. We've taken our friend to the movies, we've Talked Pictures, and we've shared how Jesus lives within our own story. Your friend is receptive to what you're saying, and you know that this could lead to something greater. But where do you go from here? What's next?

The conversation isn't over. In fact, it's just getting started! You have an opportunity before you to help nurture and guide someone toward faith and salvation in Christ Jesus. That's very exciting, but it might also feel a bit overwhelming. You may think that bringing them to faith is now your responsibility, and you're worried that you might fail. Remember, though, it's not really up to you. We know that faith is a gift from God (Ephesians 2:8), imparted by the Holy Spirit. This is God's work – not ours. He is the one who works within their heart to create this miracle. But we also know that God can use us to help guide and support others when they are brought to faith. But just like that fishing line, you don't want to reel in too hard or too fast – or the line could snap. We'll have more success if we take the time to establish trust – a key element in an enduring relationship. This comfortable pace allows us to be thinking several steps ahead. The movie may have been the initial bait on the end of that hook, but in due time we'll be able to show them so much more!

"Come and see!" We hear these words spoken time and time again in the Bible, by people whose lives were changed by an encounter with Jesus. Philip said **"Come and see"** to his doubting friend Nathanael in John 1:46. The woman at the well said it to the townspeople after she had met Jesus (John 4:29). And the angel who guarded the tomb after Jesus' resurrection said it to the women who were looking for Jesus (Matthew 28:6). *Come and see!* They knew that just hearing the story was not enough. A more personal connection was necessary. They had to move out of their comfort zone – out of the world as they had always known it – and experience Jesus for themselves.

As an Evangelist/Translator, this is your next step after the movies, the conversations, and the prayers. The best way we can "reel them in" is through an invitation to come and experience Jesus through His people and His ministries. What are some ways we can bring our friend into contact with the family of believers, especially at our own church? Think of all the things you could invite them to "come and see!"

- A church social event/party
- A Christian music concert
- A Movie Night or Game Night

- A holiday event at church (Christmas and Easter are great times to invite friends!)
- A men's or women's group
- A casual meeting with your pastor, perhaps in a non-church setting
- A small group Bible study
- A prayer group
- A worship experience

How can we help make a deeper connection between our friend's needs and the resources and blessings that the church has to offer? Consider some of these ideas:

- Have a party at your house and invite a few friends from church to informally meet your "not-yet-churched" friend
- Does your friend like sports? Many churches have teams/classes for children and adults (soccer, gymnastics, softball, karate, aerobics, etc.).
- Does your friend have a favorite hobby? Perhaps your congregation has a group that enjoys getting together for the same reason (scrapbooking club, book club, music ensemble or band, craft or quilting group, etc.).
- Invite your friend to join you in a church project that reaches out and helps those in need in the community (such as a food or clothing drive). Most people are eager to make a difference in other people's lives.
- Invite your friend to attend or help with a fundraising activity at your church. Everyone needs their car washed! Church yard sales are a great activity to pull people in. Most people are delighted to unload their old stuff for a good cause, and enjoy looking around for new treasures.
- Find a way to connect your friend's skills to the church. People love to be asked for their expertise. If your friend enjoys baking, ask if she would make a batch of cookies

for the church bake sale. Ask a techie friend to help with some of the A/V equipment at the church.

- Is your friend married? Invite them to a marriage enrichment seminar.
- Is your church affiliated with a daycare or preschool? If so, invite your friend to come by for a tour of the facilities. If not, but your friend does have young children, perhaps there's a mom's group or play group they would like to attend, or you could invite them to a parenting class or seminar.
- Youth groups are an excellent way to integrate new families into a church environment. They may offer everything from pizza parties and lock-ins to camping trips and concerts.
- Many churches now offer seminars on finances and budgeting. These classes provide a wealth of great tips and resources, regardless of one's financial situation.
- Is your friend struggling with an addiction or difficult life situation? Find a Christian support /recovery group where they can receive encouragement.

These "come and see" invitations can be made in a very casual, nonthreatening way. Of course, inviting our friends to an activity is only part of our mission. Once there, we want to help them make a positive connection with others and build new relationships. Think about the suggestions on the list above, and pray for opportunities and God's guidance. Remember to take the specific personality and needs of your friend into consideration. If one of the invitations doesn't quite resonate with your friend, try another at an opportune time. Even if the activity isn't something you would normally attend yourself (a support group, for example), you should accompany your guest to the function and help them get acquainted with others and feel comfortable.

It's great to talk about evangelism, but we're called to be people of action. When we start inviting people to "come and see," things will start to happen in their lives. Remember Nathanael, the woman at the well, and the women at the tomb. It was only after coming, seeing, and experiencing that they truly believed and were changed.

In the movie *The Bucket List*, Jack Nicholson's and Morgan Freeman's characters are both terminally ill, and both are trying to enjoy every last minute of life. Earlier in the movie, Jack resists Morgan's friendship, telling him, "Just because I told you my story, does not invite you to be a part of it!" However, in Talking Pictures, in telling your story and Jesus' story through the movie's story, you're inviting people to be a part of your life. You're inviting people to be a part of your *eternal* life! Come and see the life that lasts forever!

Perhaps the conductor on *The Polar Express* expressed it best when he said, "Seeing is believing, but sometimes the most real things in the world are the things we can't see." And while Jesus has ascended to heaven, He can be seen everywhere – all over the world – including in the hearts and lives of His followers. Jesus can be seen in our Talking Pictures, and even more so in our communities of faith where we share the Word and Sacraments. We don't want to leave a new believer to search for answers all by themselves. Share with them. Guide them. Lead them to where the answers can be found – and to those who will be there with them to share the journey of faith. We must cling to the promise that where two or more are gathered in His name, Jesus is there as well (Matthew 18:20). Come and see, and join us as we share life and eternal life together. That's our invitation. Roll 'em!

How are you Talking Pictures? Write or send me an e-mail –
I'd love to hear how God is using you as an Evangelist/
Translator! Even though I haven't met you yet, I'm praying
for you. Many people are praying for you! And most importantly, remember that Jesus is with you *always*, until the very
end of the age (Matthew 28:20)!

Mailing Address:
Dr. Jacob Youmans
Director, DCE Program
Associate Professor of Education
Concordia-Texas
11400 Concordia University Drive
Austin, TX 78726

Email: jacob.youmans@gmail.com

Filmography

2012. Dir. Roland Emmerich. Perf. John Cusack, Amanda Peet, Chiwetel Ejiofor, and Thandie Newton. Columbia Pictures, 2009.

300. Dir. Zack Snyder. Perf. Gerard Butler, Lena Headey, Dominic West, and David Wenham. Warner Bros. Pictures, 2006.

48 Hrs. Dir. Walter Hill. Perf. Nick Nolte, Eddie Murphy, Annette O'Toole, and Frank McRae. Paramount Pictures, 1982.

A Few Good Men. Dir. Rob Reiner. Perf. Tom Cruise, Jack Nicholson, Demi Moore, and Kevin Bacon. Castle Rock Entertainment, 1992.

A.I. Artificial Intelligence. Dir. Steven Spielberg. Perf. Haley Joel Osment, Frances O'Connor, Sam Robards, and Jake Thomas. Warner Bros. Pictures, 2001.

Aladdin. Dir. Ron Clements and John Musker. Perf. Scott Weinger, Robin Williams, Linda Larkin, and Jonathan Freeman. Walt Disney Feature Animation, 1992.

A League of Their Own. Dir. Penny Marshall. Perf. Tom Hanks, Geena Davis, Madonna, and Lori Petty. Columbia Pictures Corporation, 1992.

Aliens in the Attic. Dir. John Schultz. Perf. Carter Jenkins, Austin Robert Butler, Ashley Tisdale, and Ashley Boettcher. Twentieth Century Fox Film Corporation, 2009.

American Pie. Dir. Paul Weitz. Perf. Jason Biggs, Chris Klein, Thomas Ian Nicholas, and Alyson Hannigan. Universal Pictures, 1999.

Anger Management. Dir. Peter Segal. Perf. Adam Sandler, Jack Nicholson, Marisa Tomei, and Luis Guzmán. Revolution Studios, 2003.

Apollo 13. Dir. Ron Howard Perf. Tom Hanks, Bill Paxton, Kevin Bacon, and Gary Sinise. Universal Pictures, 1995.

A Simple Plan. Dir. Sam Raimi. Perf. Bill Paxton, Bridget Fonda, Billy Bob Thornton, and Brent Briscoe. British Broadcasting Corporation (BBC), 1998.

Australia. Dir. Baz Luhrmann Perf. Hugh Jackman, Bryan Brown, and Nicole Kidman. Twentieth Century Fox Film Corporation, 2008.

Avatar. Dir. James Cameron. Perf. Sam Worthington, Zoe Saldana, Sigourney Weaver, and Stephen Lang. Twentieth Century Fox Film Corporation, 2009.

Back to the Future. Dir. Robert Zemeckis. Perf. Michael J. Fox, Christopher Lloyd, Lea Thompson, and Crispin Glover. Universal Pictures, 1985.

Back to the Future Part II. Dir. Robert Zemeckis. Perf. Michael J. Fox, Christopher Lloyd, Lea Thompson, and Thomas F. Wilson. Universal Pictures, 1989.

Back to the Future Part III. Dir. Robert Zemeckis. Perf. Michael J. Fox, Christopher Lloyd, Lea Thompson, and Thomas F. Wilson. Universal Pictures, 1990.

Bad Boys. Dir. Michael Bay. Perf. Martin Lawrence, Will Smith, Will Knickerbocker, and Theresa Randle. Don Simpson/Jerry Bruckheimer Films, 1995.

The Basketball Diaries. Dir. Scott Kalvert. Perf. Leonardo DiCaprio, Lorraine Bracco, Marilyn Sokol, and James Madio. New Line Cinema, 1995.

Batman Begins. Dir. Christopher Nolan. Perf. Christian Bale, Michael Caine, Liam Neeson, and Katie Holmes. Warner Bros. Pictures, 2005.

Bedazzled. Dir. Harold Ramis. Perf. Brendan Fraser, Elizabeth Hurley, and Frances O'Connor. Twentieth Century Fox Film Corporation, 2000.

Bedtime Stories. Dir. Adam Shankman. Perf. Adam Sandler, Keri Russell, Guy Pearce, and Russell Brand. Gunn Films, 2008.

Black Hawk Down. Dir. Ridley Scott. Perf. Josh Hartnett, Ewan McGregor, Tom Sizemore, and Eric Bana. Revolution Studios, 2001.

Blank Check. Dir. Rupert Wainwright. Perf. Brian Bonsall, Karen Duffy, James Rebhorn, and Jayne Atkinson. Walt Disney Pictures, 1994.

The Blind Side. Dir. John Lee Hancock. Perf. Sandra Bullock, Tim McGraw, Quinton Aaron, and Jae Head. Alcon Entertainment, 2009.

Blowup. Dir. Michelangelo Antonioni. Perf. David Hemmings, Vanessa Redgrave, and Sarah Miles. Metro-Goldwyn-Mayer, 1966.

The Bourne Identity. Dir. Doug Liman. Perf. Matt Damon, Franka Potente, Chris Cooper, and Clive Owen. Universal Pictures, 2002.

The Bourne Supremacy. Dir. Paul Greengrass Perf. Matt Damon, Franka Potente, Brian Cox, and Julia Stiles. Universal Pictures, 2004.

The Bourne Ultimatum. Dir. Paul Greengrass. Perf. Matt Damon, Julia Stiles, David Strathairn, and Scott Glenn. Universal Pictures, 2007.

Braveheart. Dir. Mel Gibson. Perf. Mel Gibson, Patrick McGoohan, Angus Macfadyen, and Brendan Gleeson. Icon Entertainment International, 1995.

The Breakfast Club. Dir. John Hughes, Perf. Emilio Estevez, Paul Gleason, Anthony Michael Hall, and John Kapelos. A&M Films, 1985.

Bruce Almighty. Dir. Tom Shadyac. Perf. Jim Carrey, Morgan Freeman, Jennifer Aniston, and Philip Baker Hall. Universal Pictures, 2003.

The Bucket List. Dir. Rob Reiner. Perf. Jack Nicholson, Morgan Freeman, Sean Hayes, and Beverly Todd. Warner Bros. Pictures, 2007.

Can't Buy Me Love. Dir. Steve Rash. Perf. Patrick Dempsey, Amanda Peterson, Courtney Gains, and Seth Green. Touchstone Pictures, 1987.

Cast Away. Dir. Robert Zemeckis. Perf. Tom Hanks, Helen Hunt, Chris Noth, and Nick Searcy. Twentieth Century Fox Film Corporation, 2000.

Charlie Bartlett. Dir. Jon Poll. Perf. Anton Yelchin, Kat Dennings, Robert Downey Jr., and Tyler Hilton. Metro-Goldwyn-Mayer, 2007.

Charlie Wilson's War. Dir. Mike Nichols. Perf. Tom Hanks, Julia Roberts, Philip Seymour Hoffman, and Amy Adams. Universal Studios, 2007.

Chicken Little. Dir. Mark Dindal. Perf. Zach Braff, Garry Marshall, Joan Cusack, and Steve Zahn. Walt Disney Pictures, 2005.

The Chronicles of Narnia: Prince Caspian. Dir. Andrew Adamson. Perf. Ben Barnes, Georgie Henley, Skandar Keynes, and William Moseley. Walt Disney Pictures, 2008.

The Chronicles of Narnia: The Lion the Witch and the Wardrobe. Dir. Andrew Adamson. Perf. Georgie Henley, Skandar Keynes, William Moseley, and Anna Popplewell. Walt Disney Pictures, 2005.

City Slickers. Dir. Ron Underwood. Perf. Billy Crystal, Bruno Kirby, Daniel Stern, and Jack Palance. Castle Rock Entertainment, 1991.

Click. Dir. Frank Coraci. Perf. Adam Sandler, Kate Beckinsale, Christopher Walken, and Henry Winkler. Columbia Pictures, 2006.

Constantine. Dir. Francis Lawrence. Perf. Keanu Reeves, Rachel Weisz, Shia LaBeouf, and Djimon Hounsou. Warner Bros. Pictures, 2005.

Cop Out. Dir. Kevin Smith. Perf. Bruce Willis and Tracy Morgan. Warner Bros. Pictures, 2010.

The Curious Case of Benjamin Button. Dir. David Fincher. Perf. Brad Pitt, Cate Blanchett, Taraji P. Henson, and Julia Ormond. Paramount Pictures, 2008.

The Dark Knight. Dir. Christopher Nolan. Perf. Christian Bale, Michael Caine, Heath Ledger, and Gary Oldman. Warner Bros. Pictures, 2008.

The Day After Tomorrow. Dir. Roland Emmerich. Perf. Dennis Quaid, Jake Gyllenhaal, Emmy Rossum, and Sela Ward. Twentieth Century Fox Film Corporation, 2004.

Dead Poets Society. Dir. Peter Weir. Perf. Robin Williams, Robert Sean Leonard, Ethan Hawke, and Kurtwood Smith. Touchstone Pictures, 1989.

The Devil's Advocate. Dir. Taylor Hackford. Perf. Keanu Reeves, Al Pacino, Charlize Theron, and Jeffrey Jones. Warner Bros. Pictures, 1997.

The Devil Wears Prada. Dir. David Frankel. Perf. Anne Hathaway, Meryl Streep, Emily Blunt, and Stanley Tucci. Twentieth Century Fox Film Corporation, 2006.

Die Hard. Dir. John McTiernan. Perf. Bruce Willis, Alan Rickman, Bonnie Bedelia, and Reginald VelJohnso. Twentieth Century Fox Film Corporation, 1988.

Die Hard with a Vengeance. Dir. John McTiernan. Perf. Bruce Willis, Jeremy Irons, Samuel L. Jackson, and Larry Bryggman. Twentieth Century Fox Film Corporation, 1995.

District 9. Dir. Neill Blomkamp. Perf. Sharlto Copley, Jason Cope, and David James. TriStar Pictures, 2009.

Dogma. Dir. Kevin Smith. Perf. Ben Affleck, George Carlin, Matt Damon, and Linda Fiorentino. Lions Gate Entertainment, 1999.

Dr. Suess's How the Grinch Stole Christmas. Dir. Ron Howard. Perf. Jim Carrey, Jeffrey Tambor, Christine Baranski, and Bill Irwin. Universal Pictures, 2000.

Dude, Where's My Car? Dir. Danny Leiner. Perf. Ashton Kutcher, Seann William Scott, Jennifer Garner, and Marla Sokoloff. Twentieth Century Fox Film Corporation, 2000.

Dumb and Dumber. Dir. Peter Farrelly and Bobby Farrelly. Perf. Jim Carrey, Jeff Daniels, Lauren Holly, and Mike Starr. New Line Cinema, 2004.

End of Days. Dir. Peter Hyams. Perf. Arnold Schwarzenegger, Gabriel Byrne, Robin Tunney, and Kevin Pollak. Universal Studios, 1999.

End of the Spear. Dir Jim Hanon. Perf. Louie Leonardo, Chad Allen, Jack Guzman, and Chase Ellison. Jungle Films LLC, 2006.

Evan Almighty. Dir. Tom Shadyac. Perf. Steve Carell, Morgan Freeman, and Lauren Graham. Universal Pictures, 2007.

The Exorcist. Dir. William Friedkin. Perf. Ellen Burstyn, Linda Blair, Max von Sydow, and Jason Miller. Warner Bros. Pictures, 1973.

Fantastic Four. Dir. Tim Story. Perf. Ioan Gruffudd, Jessica Alba, Michael Chiklis, and Chris Evans. Twentieth Century Fox Film Corporation, 2005.

Finding Nemo. Dir. Andrew Stanton and Lee Unkrich. Perf. Albert Brooks, Ellen DeGeneres, Alexander Gould, and Willem Dafoe. Walt Disney Pictures, 2003.

Fireproof. Dir. Alex Kendrick. Perf. Kirk Cameron, Erin Bethea, Ken Bevel, and Stephen Dervan. Samuel Goldwyn Films, 2008.

Fools Rush In. Dir. Andy Tennant. Perf. Matthew Perry and Salma Hayek. Columbia Pictures, 1997.

For Love of the Game. Dir. Sam Raimi. Perf. Kevin Costner, Kelly Preston, John C. Reilly, and Jena Malone. Universal Studios, 1999.

Frankenstein. Dir. James Whale. Perf. Colin Clive, Mae Clarke, John Boles, and Boris Karloff. Universal Pictures, 1931.

The Game Plan. Dir. Andy Fickman. Perf. Dwayne Johnson, Madison Pettis, Kyra Sedgwick, and Morris Chestnut. Walt Disney Pictures, 2007.

Get Smart. Dir. Peter Segal. Perf. Steve Carell, Anne Hathaway, Dwayne Johnson, and Alan Arkin. Warner Bros. Pictures, 2008.

G.I. Joe: The Rise of Cobra. Dir. Stephen Sommers. Perf. Channing Tatum, Sienna Miller, Christopher Eccleston, and Joseph Gordon-Levitt. Paramount Pictures, 2009.

Gladiator. Dir. Ridley Scott. Perf. Russell Crowe, Joaquin Phoenix, Connie Nielsen, and Oliver Reed. DreamWorks Pictures, 2000.

The Godfather. Dir. Francis Ford Coppola. Perf. Marlon Brando, Al Pacino, James Caan, and Robert Duvall. Paramount Pictures, 1972.

Gone with the Wind. Dir. Victor Fleming. Perf. Clark Gable, Vivien Leigh, Leslie Howard, and Olivia de Havilland. Metro-Goldwyn-Mayer, 1939.

Groundhog Day. Dir. Harold Ramis. Perf. Bill Murray, Andie MacDowell, Chris Elliott, and Stephen Tobolowsky. Columbia Pictures, 1993.

Harry Potter and the Sorcerer's Stone. Dir. Chris Columbus. Perf. Daniel Radcliffe, Rupert Grint, Emma Watson, and Richard Harris. Warner Bros. Pictures, 2001.

He's Just Not That Into You. Dir. Ken Kwapis. Perf. Ginnifer Goodwin, Jennifer Aniston, Jennifer Connelly, and Justin Long. New Line Cinema, 2009.

High School Musical. Dir. Kenny Ortega. Perf. Zac Efron, Vanessa Hudgens, Ashley Tisdale, and Lucas Grabeel. Walt Disney Pictures, 2006.

High School Musical 2. Dir. Kenny Ortega. Perf. Zac Efron, Vanessa Hudgens, Ashley Tisdale, and Corbin Bleu. Walt Disney Pictures, 2007.

High School Musical 3: Senior Year. Dir. Kenny Ortega. Perf. Zac Efron, Vanessa Hudgens, Ashley Tisdale, and Lucas Grabeel. Walt Disney Pictures, 2008.

Hostel. Dir. Eli Roth. Perf. Jay Hernandez, Derek Richardson, Eyþór Guðjónsson, and Jennifer Lim. Screen Gems, 2006.

How to Train Your Dragon. Dir Chris Sanders and Dean DeBlois. Perf. Jay Baruchel, Gerard Butler, Christopher Mintz-Plasse, and Jonah Hill. Paramount Pictures, 2010.

I Am Legend. Dir. Francis Lawrence. Perf. Will Smith, Alice Braga, Dash Mihok, and Salli Richardson. Warner Bros. Pictures, 2007.

The Incredible Hulk. Dir. Louis Leterrier. Perf. Edward Norton, Liv Tyler, Tim Roth, and Ty Burrell. Universal Pictures, 2008.

Independence Day. Dir. Roland Emmerich. Perf. Will Smith, Bill Pullman, Jeff Goldblum, and Judd Hirsch. Twentieth Century Fox Film Corporation, 1996.

Indiana Jones and the Kingdom of the Crystal Skull. Dir. Steven Spielberg. Perf. Harrison Ford, Shia LaBeouf, Cate Blanchett, and Karen Allen. Paramount Pictures, 2008.

Indiana Jones and the Last Crusade. Dir. Steven Spielberg. Perf. Harrison Ford, Sean Connery, Alison Doody, and Denholm Elliott. Paramount Pictures, 1989.

Indiana Jones and the Temple of Doom. Dir. Steven Spielberg. Perf. Harrison Ford, Kate Capshaw, and Jonathan Ke Quan. Paramount Pictures, 1984.

Into the Wild. Dir. Sean Penn. Perf. Emile Hirsch, Marcia Gay Harden, William Hurt, and Jena Malone. Paramount Vantage, 2007.

Invincible. Dir. Ericson Core. Perf. Mark Wahlberg and Greg Kinnear. Walt Disney Pictures, 2006.

I, Robot. Dir. Alex Proyas. Perf. Will Smith, Bridget Moynahan, Bruce Greenwood, and James Cromwell. Twentieth Century Fox Film Corporation, 2004.

Jaws. Dir. Steven Spielberg. Perf. Roy Scheider, Richard Dreyfuss, Robert Shaw, and Lorraine Gary. Universal Pictures, 1975.

Jerry Maguire. Dir. Cameron Crowe. Perf. Tom Cruise, Cuba Gooding, Jr., Renée Zellweger, and Jonathan Lipnicki. TriStar Pictures, 1996.

Jurassic Park. Dir. Steven Spielberg. Perf. Sam Neill, Laura Dern, Jeff Goldblum, and Richard Attenborough. Universal Pictures, 1993.

King Arthur. Dir. Antoine Fuqua. Perf. Clive Owen, Keira Knightley, Ioan Gruffudd, and Mads Mikkelsen. Touchstone Pictures, 2004.

The Kiss. Dir. William Heise. Perf. May Irwin and John Rice. Thomas A. Edison, Inc., 1896.

Kiss the Girls. Dir. Gary Fleder. Perf. Morgan Freeman, Ashley Judd, and Cary Elwes. Paramount Pictures, 1997.

Lethal Weapon. Dir. Richard Donner. Perf. Danny Glover, Mel Gibson, Gary Busey, and Mitchell Ryan. Warner Bros. Studios, 1987.

Lethal Weapon 2. Dir. Richard Donner. Perf. Danny Glover, Mel Gibson, Joe Pesci, and Joss Ackland. Warner Bros. Studios, 1989.

Lethal Weapon 3. Dir. Richard Donner. Perf. Danny Glover, Mel Gibson, Joe Pesci, and Rene Russo. Warner Bros. Studios, 1992.

Lethal Weapon 4. Dir. Richard Donner. Perf. Danny Glover, Mel Gibson, Joe Pesci, and Rene Russo. Warner Bros. Studios, 1998.

The Lion King. Dir. Roger Allers and Rob Minkoff. Perf. Matthew Broderick, Jeremy Irons, James Earl Jones, and Jonathan Taylor Thomas. Buena Vista Pictures, 1994.

Live Free or Die Hard. Dir. Len Wiseman. Perf. Bruce Willis, Justin Long, Timothy Olyphant, and Maggie Q. Twentieth Century Fox Film Corporation, 2007.

The Lord of the Rings: The Fellowship of the Ring. Dir. Peter Jackson. Perf. Elijah Wood, Ian McKellen, Viggo Mortensen, and Sean Bean. New Line Cinema, 2001.

The Lord of the Rings: The Return of the King. Dir. Peter Jackson. Perf. Elijah Wood, Ian McKellen, Viggo Mortensen, and Sean Bean. New Line Cinema, 2003.

The Lord of the Rings: The Two Towers. Dir. Peter Jackson. Perf. Elijah Wood, Sean Astin, Andy Serkis, and Viggo Mortensen. New Line Cinema, 2002.

Lost in Space. Dir. Stephen Hopkins. Perf. William Hurt, Mimi Rogers, Lacey Chabert, and Heather Graham. New Line Cinema, 1998.

Luther. Dir. Eric Till. Perf. Joseph Fiennes, Alfred Molina, Jonathan Firth, and Claire Cox. Metro-Goldwyn-Mayer, 2003.

Marley and Me. Dir. David Frankel. Owen Wilson, Jennifer Aniston, Eric Dane, and Kathleen Turner. Twentieth Century Fox Film Corporation, 2008.

Martin Luther. Dir. Irving Pichel. Perf. Niall MacGinnis. De Rochemont/Lutheran Productions, 1953.

The Matrix. Dir. Andrew Paul Wachowski and Laurence Wachowski. Perf. Keanu Reeves, Laurence Fishburne, Carrie-Anne Moss, and Hugo Weaving. Warner Bros. Pictures, 1999.

The Matrix Reloaded. Dir. Andrew Paul Wachowski and Laurence Wachowski. Perf. Keanu Reeves, Laurence Fishburne, Carrie-Anne Moss, and Hugo Weaving. Warner Bros. Pictures, 2003.

The Matrix Revolutions. Dir. Andrew Paul Wachowski and Laurence Wachowski. Perf. Keanu Reeves, Laurence Fishburne, Carrie-Anne Moss, and Hugo Weaving. Warner Bros. Pictures, 2003.

Mean Girls. Dir. Mark Waters. Perf. Lindsay Lohan, Rachel McAdams, Lacey Chabert, and Amanda Seyfried. Paramount Pictures, 2004.

Meet the Fockers. Dir. Jay Roach. Perf. Robert De Niro, Ben Stiller, Dustin Hoffman, and Barbra Streisand. Universal Studios, 2004.

Meet the Parents. Dir. Jay Roach. Perf. Robert De Niro, Ben Stiller, Teri Polo, and Blythe Danner. Universal Studios, 2000.

Millions. Dir. Danny Boyle. Perf. Alexander Nathan Etel and Lewis McGibbon. Fox Searchlight Pictures, 2004.

My Big Fat Greek Wedding. Dir. Joel Zwick. Perf. Nia Vardalos, John Corbett, Lainie Kazan, and Michael Constantine. IFC Films, 2002.

Napoleon Dynamite. Dir. Jared Hess. Perf. Jon Heder, Jon Gries, Efren Ramirez, and Tina Majorino. Fox Searchlight Pictures, 2004.

National Lampoon's Christmas Vacation. Dir. Jeremiah Chechik. Perf. Chevy Chase, Beverly D'Angelo, Juliette Lewis, and Johnny Galecki. Warner Bros. Pictures, 1989.

National Lampoon's European Vacation. Dir. Amy Heckerling. Perf. Chevy Chase, Beverly D'Angelo, Dana Hill, and Jason Lively. Warner Bros. Pictures, 1985.

National Lampoon's Vacation. Dir. Harold Ramis. Perf. Chevy Chase, Beverly D'Angelo, Anthony Michael Hall, and Dana Barron. Warner Bros. Pictures, 1983.

National Lampoon's Vegas Vacation. Dir. Jeremiah Chechik. Perf. Chevy Chase, Beverly D'Angelo, Ethan Embry, and Marisol Nichols. Warner Bros. Pictures, 1997.

The Nativity Story. Dir. Catherine Hardwicke. Perf. Keisha Castle-Hughes and Shohreh Aghdashloo. New Line Cinema, 2006.

Natural Born Killers. Dir. Oliver Stone. Perf. Woody Harrelson, Juliette Lewis, Robert Downey, Jr., and Tommy Lee Jones. Warner Bros. Pictures, 1994.

The New Guy. Dir. Ed Decter. Perf. DJ Qualls, Lyle Lovett, Eddie Griffin, and Eliza Dushku. Columbia Pictures, 2002.

Night at the Museum. Dir. Shawn Levy. Perf. Ben Stiller, Carla Gugino, Dick Van Dyke, and Mickey Rooney. Twentieth Century Fox Film Corporation, 2006.

Ocean's Eleven. Dir. Steven Soderbergh. Perf. George Clooney, Brad Pitt, Matt Damon, and Andy Garcia. Warner Bros. Pictures, 2001.

Oh, God! Dir. Carl Reiner. Perf. John Denver, George Burns, Teri Garr, and Donald Pleasence. Warner Bros. Pictures, 1977.

Oh, God! Book II. Dir. Gilbert Cates. Perf. George Burns, Suzanne Pleshette, and David Birney. Warner Bros. Pictures, 1980.

Oh, God! You Devil. Dir. Paul Bogart. Perf. George Burns, Ted Wass, Ron Silver, and Roxanne Hart. Warner Bros. Pictures, 1984.

Overboard. Dir. Garry Marshall. Perf. Goldie Hawn, Kurt Russell, Edward Herrmann, and Katherine Helmond. Metro-Goldwyn-Mayer, 1987.

The Passion of the Christ. Dir. Mel Gibson. Perf. James Caviezel, Maia Morgenstern, Monica Bellucci, and Hristo Naumov Shopov. Newmarket Films, 2004.

Patch Adams. Dir. Tom Shadyac. Perf. Robin Williams, Philip Seymour Hoffman, and Monica Potter. Universal Studios, 1998.

Patton. Dir. Franklin J. Schaffner. Perf. George C. Scott, Karl Malden, Michael Bates, and Karl Michael Vogler. Twentieth Century Fox Film Corporation, 1970.

Pirates of the Caribbean: At Worlds End. Dir. Gore Verbinski. Perf. Johnny Depp, Orlando Bloom, Keira Knightley, and Chow Yun-Fat. Walt Disney Pictures, 2007.

Pirates of the Caribbean: Curse of the Black Pearl. Dir. Gore Verbinski. Perf. Johnny Depp, Orlando Bloom, Keira Knightley, and Geoffrey Rush. Walt Disney Pictures, 2003.

Pirates of the Caribbean: Dead Man's Chest. Dir. Gore Verbinski. Perf. Johnny Depp, Orlando Bloom, Keira Knightley, and Bill Nighy. Walt Disney Pictures, 2006.

The Polar Express. Dir. Robert Zemeckis. Perf. Daryl Sabara, Nona Gaye, Jimmy Bennett, and Tom Hanks. Warner Bros. Pictures, 2004.

The Princess Bride. Dir. Rob Reiner. Perf. Cary Elwes, Robin Wright, Mandy Patinkin, and Chris Sarandon. Twentieth Century Fox Film Corporation, 1987.

The Program. Dir. David S. Ward. Perf. James Caan, Halle Berry, Omar Epps, and Craig Sheffer. Touchstone Pictures, 1993.

Remember the Titans. Dir. Boaz Yakin. Perf. Denzel Washington, Will Patton, Wood Harris, and Ryan Hurst. Walt Disney Pictures, 2000.

Running Scared. Dir. Peter Hyams. Perf. Gregory Hines, Billy Crystal, and Jimmy Smits. Metro-Goldwyn-Mayer, 1986.

Saving Private Ryan. Dir. Steven Spielberg. Perf. Tom Hanks, Edward Burns, Matt Damon, and Tom Sizemore. Paramount Pictures, 1998.

Saw. Dir. James Wan. Perf. Leigh Whannell, Cary Elwes, Danny Glover, and Monica Potter. Lions Gate Entertainment, 2004.

Scrooged. Dir. Richard Donner. Perf. Bill Murray, Karen Allen, John Forsythe, and Bobcat Goldthwait. Paramount Pictures, 1988.

Se7en. Dir. David Fincher. Perf. Brad Pitt, Morgan Freeman, Gwyneth Paltrow, and Kevin Spacey. New Line Cinema, 1995.

The Shawshank Redemption. Dir. Frank Darabont. Perf. Tim Robbins and Morgan Freeman. Columbia Pictures, 1994.

Signs. Dir. M. Night Shyamalan. Perf. Mel Gibson, Joaquin Phoenix, Rory Culkin, and Abigail Breslin. Touchstone Pictures, 2002.

The Sixth Sense. Dir. M. Night Shyamalan. Perf. Bruce Willis, Haley Joel Osment, Toni Collette, and Olivia Williams. Hollywood Pictures, 1999.

Slumdog Millionaire. Dir. Danny Boyle. Perf. Dev Patel, Freida Pinto, Madhur Mittal, and Anil Kapoor. Fox Searchlight Pictures, 2008.

Spider-Man. Dir. Sam Raimi. Perf. Tobey Maguire, Willem Dafoe, Kirsten Dunst, and James Franco. Columbia Pictures, 2002.

Spider-Man 2. Dir. Sam Raimi. Perf. Tobey Maguire, Kirsten Dunst, James Franco, and Alfred Molina. Columbia Pictures, 2004.

Spider-Man 3. Dir. Sam Raimi. Perf. Tobey Maguire, Kirsten Dunst, James Franco, and Topher Grace. Columbia Pictures, 2007.

Star Trek. Dir. J. J. Abrams. Perf. John Cho, Ben Cross, Bruce Greenwood, and Simon Pegg. Paramount Pictures, 2009.

Star Wars. Dir. George Lucas. Perf. Mark Hamill, Harrison Ford, Carrie Fisher, and Peter Cushing. Twentieth Century Fox Film Corporation, 1977.

Star Wars: Episode I – The Phantom Menace. Dir. George Lucas. Perf. Liam Neeson, Ewan McGregor, Natalie Portman, and Jake Lloyd. Twentieth Century Fox Film Corporation, 1999.

Star Wars: Episode II – Attack of the Clones. Dir. George Lucas. Perf. Ewan McGregor, Hayden Christensen, Natalie Portman, and Samuel L. Jackson. Twentieth Century Fox Film Corporation, 2002.

Star Wars: Episode III – Revenge of the Sith. Dir. George Lucas. Perf. Ewan McGregor, Hayden Christensen, Natalie Portman, and Ian McDiarmid. Twentieth Century Fox Film Corporation, 2005.

Star Wars: Episode V – The Empire Strikes Back. Dir. Irvin Kershner. Perf. Mark Hamill, Harrison Ford, Carrie Fisher, and Billy Dee Williams. Twentieth Century Fox Film Corporation, 1980.

Star Wars: Episode VI – Return of the Jedi. Dir. Richard Marquand. Perf. Mark Hamill, Harrison Ford, Carrie Fisher, and Billy Dee Williams. Twentieth Century Fox Film Corporation, 1983.

Step Brothers. Dir. Adam McKay. Perf. Will Ferrell, John C. Reilly, Richard Jenkins, and Mary Steenburgen. Columbia Pictures, 2008.

Stepmom. Dir. Chris Columbus. Perf. Julia Roberts, Susan Sarandon, Ed Harris, and Jena Malone. Columbia Pictures, 1998.

Taken. Dir. Pierre Morel. Perf. Liam Neeson, Famke Janssen, Maggie Grace, and Xander Berkeley. Twentieth Century Fox Film Corporation, 2008.

Talladega Nights: The Ballad of Ricky Bobby. Dir. Adam McKay. Perf. Will Ferrell, John C. Reilly, Leslie Bibb, and Sacha Baron Cohen. Columbia Pictures, 2006.

Tango and Cash. Dir. Andrei Konchalovsky. Perf. Sylvester Stallone, Kurt Russell, Jack Palance, and Teri Hatcher. Warner Bros. Pictures, 1989.

The Ten Commandments. Dir. Cecil B. Demille. Perf. Charlton Heston, Yul Brynner, Anne Baxter, and Edward G. Robinson. Paramount Pictures, 1956.

There's Something about Mary. Dir. Bobby Farrelly and Peter Farrelly. Perf. Cameron Diaz, Matt Dillon, Ben Stiller, and Chris Elliott. Twentieth Century Fox Film Corporation, 1998.

Titanic. Dir. James Cameron. Perf. Leonardo DiCaprio, Kate Winslet, Billy Zane, and Kathy Bates. Twentieth Century Fox Film Corporation, 1997.

To Save a Life. Dir. Brian Baugh. Perf. Randy Wayne, Deja Kreutzberg, Joshua Wiegel, and Sean Michael Afable. Samuel Goldwyn Films, 2010.

Transformers: Revenge of the Fallen. Dir. Michael Bay. Perf. Shia LaBeouf, Megan Fox, John Turturro, and Ramon Rodriguez. Paramount Pictures, 2009.

The Truman Show. Dir. Peter Weir. Perf. Jim Carrey, Laura Linney, Ed Harris, and Noah Emmerich. Paramount Pictures, 1998.

Unbreakable. Dir. M. Night Shyamalan. Perf. Bruce Willis, Samuel L. Jackson, Robin Wright Penn, and Spencer Treat Clark. Touchstone Pictures, 2000.

Varsity Blues. Dir. Brian Robbins. Perf. James Van Der Beek, Amy Smart, Paul Walker, and Ali Larter. Paramount Pictures, 1999.

V for Vendetta. Dir. James McTeigue. Perf. Hugo Weaving, Natalie Portman, Stephen Rea, and Stephen Fry. Warner Bros. Pictures, 2005.

The Village. Dir. M. Night Shyamalan. Perf. Joaquin Phoenix, Bryce Dallas Howard, Adrien Brody, and William Hurt. Touchstone Pictures, 2004.

Wall Street. Dir. Oliver Stone. Perf. Michael Douglas, Charlie Sheen, Daryl Hannah, and Martin Sheen. Twentieth Century Fox Film Corporation, 1987.

We Are Marshall. Dir. Joseph McGinty Nichol. Perf. Matthew McConaughey, Matthew Fox, Anthony Mackie, and Kate Mara. Warner Bros. Pictures, 2006.

We Were Soldiers. Dir. Randall Wallace. Perf. Mel Gibson, Madeleine Stowe, Sam Elliott, and Greg Kinnear. Paramount Pictures, 2002.

The Wizard of Oz. Dir. Victor Fleming. Perf. Judy Garland, Frank Morgan, Ray Bolger, and Bert Lahr. Metro-Goldwyn-Mayer, 1939.

Mr. Woodcock. Dir. Craig Gillespie. Perf. Seann William Scott, Billy Bob Thornton, Susan Sarandon, and Ethan Suplee. New Line Cinema 2007.

Television Shows Referenced

American Idol: The Search for a Superstar. Prod. Nigel Lythgoe, Ken Warwick, and Cecile Frot-Coutaz. Fox. 2002.

The A-Team. Prod. Stephen J. Cannell and Frank Lupo. NBC. 1987.

Get Smart. Prod. Leonard B. Stern and Arne Sultan. NBC. 1965.

G.I. Joe: A Real American Hero. Prod. Joe Bacal, David H. DePatie (season 1), Margaret Loesch (season 2), Tom Griffin, and Lee Gunther. Claster Television. 1985.

The Simpsons. Prod. Al Jean, Ian Maxtone-Graham, John Frink, James L. Brooks, Matt Groening, Matt Selman, and Sam Simon. Fox. 1989.

Star Trek: The Next Generation. Prod. Gene Roddenberry, Rick Berman, and Michael Piller. CBS. 1987.

Who Wants to Be a Millionaire? Prod. Michael Davies, Leigh Hampton, Meredith Vieira, and Rich Sirop. ABC. 1999.